JESUS

Who is He?

RANDY GENTILLE

Copyright Page

Contact: Randy Gentille @ rsgentille@icloud.com

"No greater beauty
~ no greater love
could I share with you,
my beloved family and friends,
than the greatest Treasure
of my heart ~ Jesus!"

"May Jesus become and remain your
greatest Treasure"

~ RANDY GENTILLE

SPECIAL THANKS!

A very warm thanks and appreciation to Monique Rosario for the front and back cover design, her valuable input, and her loving friendship and support!

Above all, I offer my utmost thanks and praise to Jesus, our beautiful Savior, who gives us THE reason and so many other reasons to sing and rejoice – to whom, with my whole heart, I dedicate this book. We love Him because He first loved us - And, oh how He loves us!

PREFACE

"Lord, remind me how brief my time on earth will be. Remind me that my days are numbered — how fleeting my life is. You have made my life no longer than the width of my hand. My entire lifetime is just a moment to you; at best, each of us is but a breath."
— *Psalm 39:4-5 (NLT)*

"How do you know what your life will be like tomorrow? Your life is like the morning fog — it's here a little while, then it's gone."
— *James 4:14 (NLT)*

In light of these 2 verses and because none of us are guaranteed tomorrow, please ponder these two questions.

If I were to die today, do I know - for sure - where I would go?

And if I were to die today and I stood before God, and He were to ask me, "Why should I allow you into my Kingdom?" What would I say?

The very heart of this book is to help prepare us for when we do stand before God, because He will already know our answer - for He sees the innermost depths of our heart!

Prepare your heart now - "today is the day of salvation". Always keep in mind that - tomorrow may just be too late.

JESUS Who is He? is based on this Scripture.

When Jesus came to the region of Caesarea Philippi, He asked His disciples, "Who do people say that the Son of Man is?"

"Well", they replied, "some say John, the Baptist, some say Elijah, and others say Jeremiah or one of the other prophets."

Then He asked them, "But who do you say that I am?"
Simon Peter answered, "You are... (to be continued)
— Matthew 16:13-16 (NLT)

MY PRAYER
A Request for This Appeal

Abba Father, my heart cries out to You, my King. Father, Your Word says that we are ambassadors for Your Son, Jesus – and that through us, You make Your appeal to those who are lost, to those who have yet to experience the wonder and the joy of knowing You and Your beautiful salvation.

My heart's cry and prayer for this appeal is that it would bring much glory and honor to You, my King – and that it would bring true salvation to all who read it.

Holy Spirit, please anoint this appeal and all those who share the wonderful Gospel that is represented in these pages. Please anoint the heart of all who read this – of those who have yet to experience You as Savior and Lord. Please open their eyes to see Your wonder, Your glory, and Your truth.

May we all see You, Jesus, as You truly are – beautiful, glorious, and full of wonder and grace. May we, together, enjoy You now, until that wonderful day when we see You face to face in all Your glory, in all Your majesty, in all Your beauty

– to forever be in Your Presence, which is, indeed, the fullness of joy.

I ask now, my Father, Your blessing and Your anointing on this appeal in the name of Jesus, to the glory of God, the Father, in the power of Your Holy Spirit.

PRAYER CARD

Father, I pray for this person now. I ask You to flood their heart with Your light. I lovingly stand in the gap and intercede now for this soul – a soul that You so intensely and intimately love. Holy Spirit, as this person reads this appeal, please anoint their heart and eyes to see the wonderful salvation that You have provided through the precious blood of Jesus. May this person experience the wonderful rebirth, which is only made possible through You, Holy Spirit. Save now, Oh Lord – I pray in the name of Jesus.

Name:

_____

Note** This page is meant to be taken out of the book for you to keep - as a reminder to pray for this person with whom you are sharing this book - and the love of Jesus.

JESUS Who is He?

CONTENTS

INTRODUCTION

A Sure Reality

You will live forever! Although your body will some day die and you will find your present life a thing of the past, your spirit and soul will live for eternity. You were created in the image of God, and because God is Love, He created you to enjoy Him and for Him to enjoy you - forever. He so loves you and desires a close relationship and intimate fellowship with you.

He has made *every* provision for you, in Jesus, for that to be a reality. Nevertheless, you have free will and must choose Jesus and the salvation He provides for you. Jesus is the *key - He gave His all for you.* Trust in Him.

What we do with these questions in our lifetime, a lifetime that God has so graciously given us, will determine how and where we will spend our eternity.

Search your heart - your deepest thoughts - How do you answer these questions?

Who is Jesus? Who is Jesus to me? What will I do with this Jesus? You have no choice but to choose.

In these questions lie not only the mysteries of the universe and of life itself, but also the mysteries of *the deepest* questions and longings of *your* heart. Who am I really? What is my purpose here on this earth? What is my life really all about? What should I do with my life?

The whole purpose of this study, *or appeal*, if you will, is to help as many people as possible search out and really understand just **who this Jesus is** - and why He should be the most important person in their lives. Please, my friend, search this out – this is the most important thing that you will ever do in your life. Your eternity really does depend on it.

Allow me, please, to introduce into your sphere of thinking, a very *bold* statement of facts. One designed to *captivate your attention,* one which should totally rock your world – or, at the very least – your curiosity.

A specific day is coming - *a day like no other day. Every* person who ever lived, including you and me, will be present for this most incredible and awesome event. It is *the day* in which *every* knee will bow and *every* tongue will confess that Jesus Christ is Lord. On that day, there will be only two kinds of people present: *those who are lost,* who rejected Jesus as

Savior and counted His precious blood as nothing - who will be *separated from God for all eternity*; **and those** *who have been saved and redeemed by the blood of Jesus.* All those who have put their complete trust and faith in Jesus, His precious blood, and His death on the cross, will *enjoy Him for all eternity.*

In that day, Satan will have no choice but to, finally – *against every fiber of his being* – bow his knees and confess out of his mouth that **Jesus Christ is Lord of all** – to the Glory of God the Father. All the demons of hell will have to bow their knees and confess that Jesus is Lord. All the angels of God will *joyfully* bow their knees and confess that Jesus is Lord. All the lost people who have ever lived will have to fearfully bow their knees and confess that Jesus is Lord. **Then** - *All the redeemed of the Lord – those who have been washed and have been made righteous by the blood of Jesus, throughout all generations, will willingly and joyfully worship their King, fall on their knees, and with the highest praise, confess with their mouth that Jesus Christ is Lord – to the Glory of God, the Father!*

"Therefore, God elevated Him to the place of highest honor and gave Him the name above all other names, that at the name of Jesus every knee should bow, in heaven and on earth and under the earth, and every tongue confess that Jesus Christ is Lord, to the glory of God, the Father."
— *Philippians 2:9-11 (NLT)*

It is of absolute certainty – just as certain as the air you are breathing this second – that on that day you *will* bow your knees and you *will* confess with your mouth that Jesus Christ is Lord. Only one question remains. Will you bow to Him *joyfully* - as your Savior and Lord – *or* will you bow to Him fearfully - as your Judge?

My prayer is that as you search this out, God will *flood your heart with His light,* and you will see Jesus for who He really is - a very personal Savior who really loves you! *You will most definitely want to be among the redeemed of the Lord on that day.*

"May Jesus become and remain your greatest Treasure!"

CHAPTER 1

The Everlasting Father

"For a child is born to us, a son is given to us. The government will rest upon his shoulders. And he shall be called; Wonderful Counselor, Mighty God, Everlasting Father, Prince of peace. His government and its peace will never end. He will rule with fairness and justice from the throne of his ancestor David for all eternity. The passionate commitment of the Lord of Heaven's Armies will make this happen!"
— *Isaiah 9:6-7 (NLT)*

The Jesus the world knew (then and now), was born in a manger in Bethlehem of Judea in Israel about 2000 years ago. He died a man, 33 years later, in Jerusalem on a hill called Calvary - nailed to a tree. Nobody, at least, no one with any sense at all, would dispute the fact that Jesus truly existed, was born, lived his life, and died at the very young age of 33.

The Everlasting Father

Historical records can prove all of that. To the world, Jesus was born, lived, and died like any other man. He was buried – and that was the end of it. Or was it?? He is *much, much, much* more than that! My friend, *please* search this out and *know* for yourself.

Jesus has myriad names and titles in God's Word. In the book of Isaiah, written by the prophet Isaiah, Jesus is called a Child who was born, a Son who was given, the Wonderful Counselor, the Mighty God, *the Everlasting Father,* and the Prince of Peace. This is a prophetic word given by God himself to Isaiah in the form of a vision – 680 to 700 years BC – before Jesus was ever born. Jesus is referred to as the Everlasting or Eternal Father many times and in many ways in *God's Word – the Bible – which, in fact, is God's Story – a story of redemption and salvation.* Jesus himself claimed it when he conversed with Philip about this very issue.

Philip said, "Lord show us the Father and we will be satisfied. Jesus replied, "Have I been with you all this time, Philip, and you still don't know who I am? Anyone who has seen me has seen the Father. So why are you asking me to show Him to you? Don't you believe that I am in the Father and the Father is in me? The words I speak are not my own, but the Father who lives in me does His work through me. Just believe that I am in the Father and the Father is in me. Or at least believe because of the work you have seen me do!"
— John 14:8-11 (NLT)

Sometime later, after his amazing conversion, the Apostle Paul reveals to the Hebrew believers in the first chapter of his letter to the Hebrews, that Jesus is the radiance of God's glory and the exact representation of the Father's nature.

Paul also exhorted the Philippian believers to have the same attitude that Jesus embraced:

"You must have the same attitude that Christ Jesus had. Though he was God, he did not think of equality with God as something to cling to. Instead, he gave up his divine privileges; he took the humble position of a slave and was born as a human being. When he appeared in human form, he humbled himself in obedience to God and died a criminal's death on a cross."
— Philippians 2:5-8 (NLT)

The truths that we encounter in God's Word will not always make sense to our human mind. They must be mixed with faith and be believed in the heart. The Holy Spirit makes that possible, if we have a desire and an open heart to know the truth.

CHAPTER 2

God, the Father, Son, and Holy Spirit

In the book of 1 John chapter 5, it is made clear that there are three Persons in the Trinity – for it states that there are three that bear record in heaven – the Father, the Word (Jesus), and the Holy Spirit; and these three are one.

(Jesus speaking) – *"But when the Father sends the Advocate as my representative – that is, the Holy Spirit – He will teach you everything and will remind you of everything that I have told you." John 14:26 (NLT)*

"Long ago God spoke many times and in many ways to our ancestors through the prophets. And now in these final days, he has spoken to us through His Son. God promised everything to the Son as an inheritance, and through the Son He created

the universe. The Son radiates God's own Glory and expresses the very character of God, and He sustains everything by the mighty power of his command. When He had cleansed us from our sins, he sat down in the place of honor at the right hand of the Majestic God in heaven."
— *Hebrews 1:1-3 (NLT)*

It really makes no difference what anyone might say or claim, God's Word is extremely clear about who this Jesus is, why He was born, and what He came to accomplish for you and me. God's Word declares that Jesus, before he was born as man, existed in eternity as God.

"Then God said, "Let Us make man in Our image, according to Our likeness; and let them rule over the fish of the sea and over the birds of the sky and over the cattle and over all the earth, and over every creeping thing that creeps on the earth." God created man in His own image, in the image of God He created him; male and female He created them."
— *Genesis 1:26-27 (NASB)*

God, in this passage, is revealing and making known to us the mystery of the Godhead. God is *ONE GOD – THREE PERSONS* – God, the Father, God, the Son, and God, the Holy Spirit. They co-exist eternally in perfect community – in perfect harmony – being the perfect relational God. The next chapter provides even more clarification. That is why Jesus was able to truthfully say to Philip:

"... He who has seen Me has seen the Father."
— *John 14:9 (NASB)*

Although very mysterious, because it is impossible for the human mind to fully comprehend and make sense of, it is altogether possible for the human heart to truly accept and truly believe - *by faith.*

"And it is impossible to please God without faith. Anyone who wants to come to him must believe that God exists and that he rewards those who sincerely seek him."
— *Hebrews 11:6 (NLT)*

So, a heart that is open and seeking the truth is all the Holy Spirit needs to shed His light. My friend, I ask that as you search out who this Jesus is – please ask the Holy Spirit to open the eyes of your heart, so that you can believe and receive Jesus by faith. Even faith is a gift of God.

"For by grace you have been saved through faith; and that not of yourselves, it is the gift of God; not as a result of works, so that no one may boast."
— *Ephesians 2:8-9 (NASB)*

CHAPTER 3

Creator of All Things

Because God's Word is always the final authority and our only true plumbline, let's start again with some of the Scriptures about the Creation account as they relate to God, the Father, the Son, and the Holy Spirit.

"In the beginning, God created the heavens and the earth. The earth was without form and void, and darkness was over the face of the deep. And the Spirit of God was hovering over the face of the waters."
— *Genesis 1:1-2 (ESV)*

"Then God said, "Let us make man in our image, after our likeness. And let them have dominion over the fish of the sea and over the birds of the heavens and over the livestock and over all the earth and over every creeping thing that creeps on

the earth." So God created man in his own image, in the image of God he created him; male and female he created them."
— *Genesis 1:26-27 (ESV)*

Many generations later, with crystal clarity, the Gospel of John declares that the Word and Jesus are, in fact, one and the same and that He created all things.

"In the beginning was the Word, and the Word was with God, and the Word was God. He was in the beginning with God. All things were made through him, and without him was not any thing made that was made. In him was life, and the life was the light of men. And the Word became flesh and dwelt among us, and we have seen his glory, glory as of the only Son from the Father, full of grace and truth."
— *John 1:1-4, 14 (ESV)*

The book of Colossians then sheds even more light on the fact that Jesus IS the visible image of the invisible God.

"For He rescued us from the domain of darkness, and transferred us to the kingdom of His beloved Son, in whom we have redemption, the forgiveness of sins.

He is the image of the invisible God, the firstborn of all creation. For by Him all things were created, both in the heavens and on earth, visible and invisible, whether thrones or dominions or rulers or authorities—all things have been created through Him and for Him. He is before all things, and in Him all things hold together.

He is also head of the body, the church; and He is the beginning, the firstborn from the dead, so that He Himself will come to have first place in everything. For it was the Father's good pleasure for all the fullness to dwell in Him, and through Him to reconcile all things to Himself, having made peace through the blood of His cross; through Him, I say, whether things on earth or things in heaven."
— *Colossians 1:13-20 (NASB)*

How can anyone read these passages of Scripture and still not believe? Jesus is supreme. He is our everything. The Word of God reveals and makes known everything that we need to know about God's plan of salvation and through *whom* this was made possible. We need but search it out.

Paul, the apostle wrote these words to the church at Colossae about 60 years after the death and resurrection of Jesus. You will also see many other similar letters written to the other churches – Rome – Ephesus – Philippi – Galatia , etc. Paul was sent by God to the Gentiles (anyone who was not Jewish) to make known the Good News of salvation for all people, Jew and Gentile alike. *(You can read of Paul's extraordinary experience and how God radically changed his life in the Book of Acts - chapter 9).* Paul writes of this **"mysterious plan".** **The Good News** *is that* Jesus is the Creator of all things and He is also the Savior of all who will come to Him in faith believing.

To all those who truly want to know Him, the Holy Spirit will open your eyes and your heart, in a miraculous way – so

Creator of All Things

you can, for maybe the first time, see the glorious light of the Gospel – or Good News. You just need to ask.

CHAPTER 4

A Just and Holy God

66 *T*hey came to a place named Gethsemane; and He *said to His disciples, "Sit here until I have prayed." And He took with Him Peter and James and John, and began to be very distressed and troubled. And He *said to them, "My soul is deeply grieved to the point of death; remain here and keep watch." And He went a little beyond them, and fell to the ground and began to pray that if it were possible, the hour might pass Him by. And He was saying, "Abba! Father! All things are possible for You; remove this cup from Me; yet not what I will, but what You will." And He *came and *found them sleeping, and *said to Peter, "Simon, are you asleep? Could you not keep watch for one hour? Keep watching and praying that you may not come into temptation; the spirit is willing, but the flesh is weak."*
— Mark 14:32-38 (NASB)

A Just and Holy God

In Luke's Gospel account – (after he had prayed twice)

"Now an angel from heaven appeared to Him, strengthening Him. And being in agony He was praying very fervently; and His sweat became like drops of blood, falling down upon the ground."
— *Luke 22:43-44 (NASB)*

So why did Jesus have to go through all of this? Why was it God, the Father's will for Jesus to suffer and die the awful and excruciating way that He did?

It is very clear in Scripture that there was absolutely no other option. There was no other way for fallen man to be redeemed and reconciled to God. This fact alone makes it unmistakably clear that no one would ever be able to get into Heaven by good works or by simply being good enough. This completely shatters most people's false hope of self-achieved salvation! The "good outweighs the bad" theory is found nowhere in Scripture and consequently, is one of the most effective lies of Satan. The awful road to Calvary – to the cross – was the only way. But, why?

In early October of 2006, I received a phone call that my mother was dying. So, I flew to Ohio, from California, to be with her and to love her to the end. She had been diagnosed, for the umpteenth time, with cancer. The prognosis – very bleak. She was a fighter and had beat cancer several times, but this time was different. Cancer is a horrible, horrible condition – tenacious, unmerciful and unrelenting. It cares not who it destroys – 80 years old or 6 years old – it makes no difference. It is an awful, degenerative, destructive force. Left untreated or, should I say - uncured, it will surely destroy anyone or anything in its path. She died on Oct. 26, 2006.

One and a half months later, my father was diagnosed with a different, but still deadly form of cancer. In mid-December I flew to Ohio, once again, to love and care for my father. He died a very short time later on Dec. 18, 2006. In less than 2 months time, cancer had ruthlessly claimed the precious lives of two very beautiful people – my parents – who I dearly loved.

I tell you this story because cancer is probably the closest thing we can use to describe, and possibly understand, another dreaded and horrible condition – SIN. Sin is, without a doubt, the most horrible, destructive, tenacious, unmerciful, and unrelenting condition known to mankind. It is at the very core of all sickness, all disease, and every evil known to mankind. Sin left untreated or uncured – or rather unforgiven – leads only to death and destruction and ultimately hell. Pretty bleak, huh? Sin is a condition with which every man and every woman must deal. Why?? God's Word is extremely clear about the issue of sin. Very simply – God's Word concludes that everyone is sinful - guilty as charged - every one of us! And *we* can't make this right.

"As it is written: "None is righteous, no, not one; no one understands; no one seeks for God. All have turned aside; together they have become worthless; no one does good, not even one." "Their throat is an open grave; they use their tongues to deceive." "The venom of asps is under their lips." "Their mouth is full of curses and bitterness." "Their feet are swift to shed blood; in their paths are ruin and misery, and the

A Just and Holy God

way of peace they have not known." "There is no fear of God before their eyes."

"Now we know that whatever the law says it speaks to those who are under the law, so that every mouth may be stopped, and the whole world may be held accountable to God. For by works of the law no human being will be justified in his sight, since through the law comes knowledge of sin. But now the righteousness of God has been manifested apart from the law, although the Law and the Prophets bear witness to it— the righteousness of God through faith in Jesus Christ for all who believe. For there is no distinction: for all have sinned and fall short of the glory of God."
— Romans 3:10-23 (ESV)

There is no possible way that anyone could read this portion of God's Word and say , "I have never sinned." There has never been a person born who could truthfully and rightfully claim a life without sin – totally righteous – *except one* – Jesus Christ, our Savior. Because God is a just and holy God, our sin has to be dealt with and paid for. God cannot just excuse our sins or He would no longer be just. God reveals in His Word the payment requirement for our sins.

Hebrews 9:22 teaches us that - without the shedding of blood, there is no forgiveness of sins.

(Read the whole chapter 9 of Hebrews to understand the first covenant God had with Israel concerning blood sacrifice for sin.)

This was only a foreshadow of the true and final sacrifice for sin – Jesus.

"All this is from God, who through Christ reconciled us to himself and gave us the ministry of reconciliation; that is, in Christ God was reconciling the world to himself, not counting their trespasses against them, and entrusting to us the message of reconciliation. Therefore, we are ambassadors for Christ, God making his appeal through us. We implore you on behalf of Christ, be reconciled to God. For our sake he made him to be sin who knew no sin, so that in him we might become the righteousness of God."
— *2 Corinthians 5:18-21 (ESV)*

The payment for sin had to be sacrifice. And the sacrifice had to be without spot, without blemish – perfect. This is why Jesus had to be born as a baby, live His whole life **without sin** and **then** shed His precious blood for our sins – to satisfy the righteous and just requirement of a Just and Holy God. Jesus was, still is, and will always be the only sinless, perfect person, worthy and able, and thank God, willing to pay for all the sins of all mankind.

Now, do you see why Jesus had to go through all of this? Why it was God, the Father's will for Jesus to suffer and die the awful and excruciating way that He did on the cross? Jesus was the only sinless person who ever was born in this earth – making Him the only one who could possibly pay for your sins and mine. There was absolutely no other option. The awful road to Calvary – to the cross – was indeed the only way.

A Just and Holy God

When Jesus took our place on the cross, shedding His blood for our sins, He willingly took on himself every sin of every person who had ever lived (all the way back to Adam and Eve) and of every person who would ever live after Him. He also knew that as He did that, God, the Father would turn His face away from Him – breaking the fellowship that Jesus had *always known* and *always cherished* throughout eternity. The full weight, anger and fury of God's wrath was poured out on Jesus – His only Son – for **our** sins – yours, mine and the sins of every human who ever lived. Can we understand now why Jesus said in the Garden of Gethsemane – "My soul is **crushed with grief** – to the point of death." Or why **he sweat great drops of blood – being in agony of spirit?** What was the most excruciating thing for Jesus? Could it have been the separation from God the Father?

Jesus loves me, this I know. I truly hope that *you* know this also.

Please turn to Him now, ask Him to forgive you of all your sins and wash you with His precious blood. He will change your heart and life if you truly ask Him in faith believing. He paid the full price for your sins – **so *you* can enjoy *Him* forever.**

CHAPTER 5

The Word of God Become Flesh

"*In the beginning was the Word, and the Word was with God, and the Word was God. He was in the beginning with God. All things were made through him, and without him was not any thing made that was made. In him was life, and the life was the light of men. The light shines in the darkness, and the darkness has not overcome it.*

There was a man sent from God, whose name was John. He came as a witness, to bear witness about the light, that all might believe through him. He was not the light, but came to bear witness about the light.

The true light, which gives light to everyone, was coming into the world. He was in the world, and the world was made

The Word of God Become Flesh

through him, yet the world did not know him. He came to his own, and his own people did not receive him. But to all who did receive him, who believed in his name, he gave the right to become children of God, who were born, not of blood nor of the will of the flesh nor of the will of man, but of God.

And the Word became flesh and dwelt among us, and we have seen his glory, glory as of the only Son from the Father, full of grace and truth."
— John 1:1-14 (ESV)

John, in his Gospel account, gives us probably the most profound and clear-cut claim in the Word of God -- that this Jesus is, indeed, the Word of God become flesh. *Jesus is fully God and fully man.* It shows that Jesus existed with God in eternity. He exists in perfect community – Father, Son, and Holy Spirit. Jesus was, is, and will always be God. It reveals that Jesus is, indeed, the very Word that was spoken to create all things – and the Word that holds all things together. This account is also in perfect harmony with the whole of God's Word.

Think about this. Jesus, who is God, left His glorious throne in Heaven, willingly threw off His majestic robes, relinquished all of His rights and privileges as the Creator, the God of the universe, King of kings and Lord of lords. There is none like Him. Yet, He was born as a helpless baby in a lowly manger, a stinky barn, mind you. He grew up as a child and *learned* how to build things as a carpenter's son - the God who created everything - by merely speaking. He became servant to all, even to the lowliest of all – He humbled Himself and became obedient – to the point of

24

death – even death on a cross. He, the King of Glory, was spit upon, mocked, scourged and beaten – treated as a criminal – and crucified – the lowest form of death.

"Christ redeemed us from the curse of the law by becoming a curse for us—for it is written, "Cursed is everyone who is hanged on a tree".
— *Galatians 3:13 (ESV)*

Jesus himself said that at any time He could have called ten thousand angels to deliver Him from the hands of those who were crucifying Him – yet He didn't. He opened not His mouth. You see, in God's Story of salvation and redemption, He made Himself to be the sacrifice for our sin. The Word was to become flesh – He became flesh, a man born into this world – for the sole purpose of dying. God in His Perfection and Wisdom knew that He was the only one who could redeem man – and He was so willing to do it.

Can anyone who truly understands this really walk away from that kind of love?

CHAPTER 6

The God of Love, Mercy, and Grace

"*But God, being rich in mercy, because of the great love with which he loved us, even when we were dead in our trespasses, made us alive together with Christ—by grace you have been saved— and raised us up with him and seated us with him in the heavenly places in Christ Jesus, so that in the coming ages he might show the immeasurable riches of his grace in kindness toward us in Christ Jesus. For by grace you have been saved through faith. And this is not your own doing; it is the gift of God, not a result of works, so that no one may boast. For we are his workmanship, created in Christ Jesus for good works, which God prepared beforehand, that we should walk in them.*"
— *Ephesians 2:4-10 (ESV)*

The God of Love, Mercy, and Grace

There could never be enough books written about the fact that God is Love. God is Mercy. God is Grace. He doesn't just possess these qualities, He embodies them. As God puts it – I AM.

As we discussed in the last topic, Jesus humbled himself, took on the form of a servant, willingly died a horrible, humiliating death for a world full of rebellious, selfish sinners – sinners who deserve *anything but* His love, mercy, and grace. What could possibly motivate the God of all creation? The only possible explanation is that **God is Love!** Think about it.

"For God so loved the world, that He gave His only begotten Son, that whoever believes in Him shall not perish, but have eternal life. For God did not send the Son into the world to judge the world, but that the world might be saved through Him."
— John 3:16-17 (NASB)

Oh, you had to know that verse was coming – at least at some point. There is not a more well known or more quoted verse in all the Bible than that verse – and for good reason. If there is one thing that God desperately wants **everyone** to know – is that He loves them – us – with a perfect, unfailing love. He went to the most extreme lengths to secure our salvation. He paid for it with His own precious blood. BUT we have a choice and God will never supersede our will – or our choice.

The next few verses are perhaps not quite as well known...

"He who believes in Him is not judged; he who does not believe has been judged already, because he has not believed in the

name of the only begotten Son of God. This is the judgment, that the Light has come into the world, and men loved the darkness rather than the Light, for their deeds were evil. For everyone who does evil hates the Light, and does not come to the Light for fear that his deeds will be exposed. But he who practices the truth comes to the Light, so that his deeds may be manifested as having been wrought in God."
— John 3:18-21 (NASB)

God has made every provision for your salvation – but the choice still remains yours. By just ignoring the whole matter – you are choosing not to trust in, cling to, and rely on Jesus for your salvation. Just to *"believe"* facts about God or Jesus is not the *faith* of which the Word of God speaks. (Even Satan believes in God). Faith in the Son of God involves a heart of repentance – repenting or turning from your sin and former way or "practice" of life unto God. When someone displays true, *genuine saving faith,* the Holy Spirit illuminates and changes a person's heart – this is known in God's Word as being "reborn" or "born again". This can only be the work of the Holy Spirit – when someone truly repents and trusts in, clings to, and relies on Jesus totally and completely for his or her salvation.

The Word of God clearly portrays this concept in the first part of John chapter 3, the story of Nicodemus.

"Now there was a man of the Pharisees, named Nicodemus, a ruler of the Jews; this man came to Jesus by night and said to Him, "Rabbi, we know that You have come from God as a teacher; for no one can do these signs that You do unless God

is with him." Jesus answered and said to him, "Truly, truly, I say to you, unless one is born again he cannot see the kingdom of God."

Nicodemus *said to Him, "How can a man be born when he is old? He cannot enter a second time into his mother's womb and be born, can he?" Jesus answered, "Truly, truly, I say to you, unless one is born of water and the Spirit he cannot enter into the kingdom of God. That which is born of the flesh is flesh, and that which is born of the Spirit is spirit. Do not be amazed that I said to you, 'You must be born again.' The wind blows where it wishes and you hear the sound of it, but do not know where it comes from and where it is going; so is everyone who is born of the Spirit."

Nicodemus said to Him, "How can these things be?" Jesus answered and said to him, "Are you the teacher of Israel and do not understand these things? Truly, truly, I say to you, we speak of what we know and testify of what we have seen, and you do not accept our testimony. If I told you earthly things and you do not believe, how will you believe if I tell you heavenly things? No one has ascended into heaven, but He who descended from heaven: the Son of Man. As Moses lifted up the serpent in the wilderness, even so must the Son of Man be lifted up; so that whoever believes will in Him have eternal life."
— John 3: 1-15 (NASB)

Then: For God so loved the world, that He gave His only begotten Son, that whoever believes in Him shall not perish, but have eternal life."
— *John 3:16 (NASB)*

Salvation is a supernatural gift of God – freely given and *birthed* in the heart of any man, woman, or child who truly humbles him or herself and seeks the truth in Jesus. The Holy Spirit miraculously gives them new life – a brand new heart. Unless you are born again, you cannot see the Kingdom of God. My friend, please, seek and ask -- then allow the Spirit of God to breathe His new life into you.

"Therefore if anyone is in Christ, he is a new creature; the old things passed away; behold, new things have come."
— *2 Corinthians 5:17 (NASB)*

CHAPTER 7

The Sacrifice Lamb

There are many "types and shadows" that God chose to use in the Old Testament accounts – the time beginning with the creation of the world until the birth of Jesus. Our calendar – time itself – is defined and divided by the advent or *First Coming* of this one man – Jesus Christ. BC means "before Christ" and AD (anno domini) means " in the year of the Lord" – specifically referring to the birth of Christ. The very fact that our calendar is divided and defined in this way should tell you just how extremely important this Jesus truly is.

That being said, the story of Abraham – who is known as "the friend of God" and also as "the father of many nations" – is one of those "types and shadows" that reveal the heart of God and also the plan of God – from the creation of the world.

The Sacrifice Lamb

Abraham believed God. This was credited to him as righteousness. Faith pleases God – all through the Bible and today, as well. God gave Abraham many promises – **huge** promises. One such promise was that God would make Abraham a *father of many nations,* and that his descendants would be as numerable as the stars in the sky – the sand on the shore. The only problem with that, (from a human perspective), was that when Abraham was 100 years old and Sarah was 90 years old they still had *no children.* Being way past the time of typically having children – just plain old and worn out – it would take great faith to believe this enormous promise of God. The story plays out as one would expect – God was faithful to His Word – as always – and Isaac was born. From him would come many nations – right? This is where our story picks up – with God talking to Abraham – with a very unusual request.

"Now it came about after these things, that God tested Abraham, and said to him, "Abraham!" And he said, "Here I am." He said, "Take now your son, your only son, whom you love, Isaac, and go to the land of Moriah, and offer him there as a burnt offering on one of the mountains of which I will tell you." So Abraham rose early in the morning and saddled his donkey, and took two of his young men with him and Isaac his son; and he split wood for the burnt offering, and arose and went to the place of which God had told him. On the third day Abraham raised his eyes and saw the place from a distance. Abraham said to his young men, "Stay here with the donkey, and I and the lad will go over there; and we will worship and return to you." Abraham took the wood of the burnt offering

34

and laid it on Isaac his son, and he took in his hand the fire and the knife. So the two of them walked on together. Isaac spoke to Abraham his father and said, "My father!" And he said, "Here I am, my son." And he said, "Behold, the fire and the wood, but where is the lamb for the burnt offering?" Abraham said, "God will provide for Himself the lamb for the burnt offering, my son." So the two of them walked on together.

Then they came to the place of which God had told him; and Abraham built the altar there and arranged the wood, and bound his son Isaac and laid him on the altar, on top of the wood. Abraham stretched out his hand and took the knife to slay his son. But the angel of the Lord called to him from heaven and said, "Abraham, Abraham!" And he said, "Here I am." He said, "Do not stretch out your hand against the lad, and do nothing to him; for now I know that you fear God, since you have not withheld your son, your only son, from Me." Then Abraham raised his eyes and looked, and behold, behind him a ram caught in the thicket by his horns; and Abraham went and took the ram and offered him up for a burnt offering in the place of his son. Abraham called the name of that place The Lord Will Provide, as it is said to this day, "In the mount of the Lord it will be provided."

Then the angel of the Lord called to Abraham a second time from heaven, and said, "By Myself I have sworn, declares the Lord, because you have done this thing and have not withheld your son, your only son, indeed I will greatly bless you, and I will greatly multiply your seed as the stars of the heavens and

as the sand which is on the seashore; and your seed shall possess the gate of their enemies. In your seed all the nations of the earth shall be blessed, because you have obeyed My voice."
— *Genesis 22:1-18 (NASB)*

Many, many generations later, about 68 years after the death and resurrection of Jesus, the author of the Book of Hebrews writes about this very account – in a passage that is now commonly known as the "Hall of Faith".

"By faith Abraham, when he was tested, offered up Isaac, and he who had received the promises was offering up his only begotten son; it was he to whom it was said, "In Isaac your descendants shall be called." He considered that God is able to raise people even from the dead, from which he also received him back as a type."
— *Hebrews 11:17 (NASB)*

This is an incredible story of sacrifice, faith, and obedience. Abraham was willing because, for all he knew, it was God's will for him to sacrifice his one and only son, Isaac. At this point Isaac had no children but he was, according to God, to become "many nations". Fortunately, for Abraham - *(Isaac was probably pretty relieved also!)* – God stopped him and Isaac was spared! What an amazing "type and shadow" of how God sacrificed His one and only Son, Jesus. Unlike Isaac, however, Jesus was not spared. Jesus had to be the "Sacrifice Lamb" in order for God to redeem a sinful human race back to Himself.

In the Old Testament times, they were continually offering sacrifices and burnt offerings for their sins. However, it wasn't possible that the blood of bulls, goats, and lambs could take away sins – it only "covered" their sin – until the true Lamb of God, Jesus, came and shed His blood – *once and for all.*

"First, Christ said, "You did not want animal sacrifices or sin offerings or burnt offerings or other offerings for sin, nor were you pleased with them" (though they are required by the law of Moses). Then he said, "Look, I have come to do your will." He cancels the first covenant in order to put the second into effect.

For God's will was for us to be made holy by the sacrifice of the body of Jesus Christ, once for all time.

Under the old covenant, the priest stands and ministers before the altar day after day, offering the same sacrifices again and again, which can never take away sins. But our High Priest offered himself to God as a single sacrifice for sins, good for all time. Then he sat down in the place of honor at God's right hand.

There he waits until his enemies are humbled and made a footstool under his feet. For by that one offering he forever made perfect those who are being made holy.

And the Holy Spirit also testifies that this is so. For he says, "This is the new covenant I will make with my people on that day, says the Lord: I will put my laws in their hearts, and I will write them on their minds."

The Sacrifice Lamb

Then he says, "I will never again remember their sins and lawless deeds." And when sins have been forgiven, there is no need to offer any more sacrifices."
— *Hebrews 10:8-18 (NLT)*

This is precisely what John the Baptist was referring to when he testified and boldly proclaimed in John chapter 1:

"The next day he *saw Jesus coming to him and *said, "Behold, the Lamb of God who takes away the sin of the world! This is He on behalf of whom I said, 'After me comes a Man who has a higher rank than I, for He existed before me.' I did not recognize Him, but so that He might be manifested to Israel, I came baptizing in water." John testified saying, "I have seen the Spirit descending as a dove out of heaven, and He remained upon Him. I did not recognize Him, but He who sent me to baptize in water said to me, 'He upon whom you see the Spirit descending and remaining upon Him, this is the One who baptizes in the Holy Spirit.' I myself have seen, and have testified that this is the Son of God."
— *John 1:29-34 (NASB)*

So you see, Jesus was the perfect, spotless, sinless Lamb of God – the only perfect sacrifice that could satisfy the holy requirements of a Just, Holy, and yet loving God. What could possibly motivate the God of all creation to willingly give His life for a world full of rebellious, selfish sinners? Again, the **only** possible explanation is that **God is Love**.

Isaiah prophesied about this Lamb of God who was to freely give His life – more than 600 years before Jesus was ever born. He prophesied with amazing accuracy.

"But He was pierced through for our transgressions, He was crushed for our iniquities; The chastening for our well-being fell upon Him, And by His scourging we are healed. All of us like sheep have gone astray, Each of us has turned to his own way; But the Lord has caused the iniquity of us all To fall on Him.

He was oppressed and He was afflicted, Yet He did not open His mouth; Like a lamb that is led to slaughter, And like a sheep that is silent before its shearers, So He did not open His mouth. By oppression and judgment He was taken away; And as for His generation, who considered That He was cut off out of the land of the living For the transgression of my people, to whom the stroke was due? His grave was assigned with wicked men, Yet He was with a rich man in His death, Because He had done no violence, Nor was there any deceit in His mouth.

But the Lord was pleased To crush Him, putting Him to grief; If He would render Himself as a guilt offering, He will see His offspring, He will prolong His days, And the good pleasure of the Lord will prosper in His hand. As a result of the anguish of His soul, He will see it and be satisfied; By His knowledge the Righteous One, My Servant, will justify the many, As He will bear their iniquities. Therefore, I will allot Him a portion with the great, And He will divide the booty with the strong; Because He poured out Himself to death, And was numbered

The Sacrifice Lamb

with the transgressors; Yet He Himself bore the sin of many, And interceded for the transgressors."
— *Isaiah 53:5-12 (NASB)*

Jesus said it this way:

"Greater love has no one than this, that one lay down his life for his friends."
— *John 15:13 (NASB)*

CHAPTER 8

The Way, the Truth, and the Life

"Jesus *said to him, "I am the way, and the truth, and the life; no one comes to the Father but through Me. If you had known Me, you would have known My Father also; from now on you know Him, and have seen Him."
— *John 14:6-7 (NASB)*

Jesus made many bold statements as to who He was – and who He still is today. These statements have been proved true by many signs, wonders, and miracles. To top it all off, Jesus fulfilled many, many prophesies about Himself – prophesies that were given many years and even generations before Jesus was ever physically on this earth. The ultimate sign? **Jesus boldly proclaimed, as the Scriptures had already** *foretold, that He, indeed, would die – but that three days later He would rise from the dead.*

Indeed, He did rise from the dead and was seen by more than 500 people over a space of 40 days.

"For I delivered to you as of first importance what I also received, that Christ died for our sins according to the Scriptures, and that He was buried, and that He was raised on the third day according to the Scriptures, and that He appeared to Cephas, then to the twelve. After that He appeared to more than five hundred brethren at one time, most of whom remain until now, but some have fallen asleep; then He appeared to James, then to all the apostles; and last of all, as to one untimely born, He appeared to me also. For I am the least of the apostles, and not fit to be called an apostle, because I persecuted the church of God."
— 1 Corinthians 15:3-9 (NASB)

Here is more of what Jesus revealed about himself. Anyone who can predict His own death and resurrection and *actually pull it off* is someone well worth listening to – wouldn't you say?

Jesus replied, "I Am the bread of life. Whoever comes to Me will never be hungry again. Whoever believes in Me will never be thirsty."
— John 6:35 (NLT)

"I Am the living bread that came down from heaven. Anyone who eats this bread will live forever; and this bread, which I will offer so the world may live, is my flesh."
— John 6:51 (NLT)

Jesus spoke to the people once more and said, "I Am the Light of the world. If you follow Me, you won't have to walk in darkness, because you will have the Light that leads to life"
— John 8:12 (NLT)

So He explained to them; "I tell you the truth, I Am the gate for the sheep. All who ever came before Me were thieves and robbers. But the true sheep did not listen to them. Yes, I Am the gate. Those who come in through Me will be saved!"
— John 10:7 (NLT)

"I Am the Good Shepherd. The Good Shepherd sacrifices his life for the sheep." (verse 14) "I Am the Good Shepherd; I know my own sheep, and they know me!"
— John 10:11 (NLT)

Jesus told her, "I Am the resurrection and the life. Anyone who believes in Me will live, even after dying. Everyone who lives in Me and believes in me will never die. Do you believe this, Martha?" "Yes, Lord", she told Him. "I have always believed You are the Messiah, the Son of God, the One who has come into this world from God!"
— John 11:25-27 (NLT)

The Way, the Truth, and the Life

"I am the true vine, and My Father is the vinedresser."
— John 15:1 (NASB)

"I am the vine, you are the branches; he who abides in Me and I in him, he bears much fruit, for apart from Me you can do nothing."
— John 15:5 (NASB)

Then Luke, author of the Book of Acts, gives this account of Peter and John, who, **in the name of this same Jesus,** healed a lame man by the Temple gate.

"Let it be known to all of you and to all the people of Israel, that by the name of Jesus Christ the Nazarene, whom you crucified, whom God raised from the dead—by this name this man stands here before you in good health. He is the stone which was rejected by you, the builders, but which became the chief corner stone. And there is salvation in no one else; for there is no other name under heaven that has been given among men by which we must be saved."
— Acts 4:10-12 (NASB)

CHAPTER 9

Messiah, Redeemer, and Savior

God, in His wisdom, says in His Word that faith comes by hearing – that is, hearing the Good News about Christ. So, here are a few scriptures to build faith in your heart about Jesus as Messiah, Redeemer and Savior.

"Now there was a man in Jerusalem, whose name was Simeon, and this man was righteous and devout, waiting for the consolation of Israel, and the Holy Spirit was upon him. And it had been revealed to him by the Holy Spirit that he would not see death before he had seen the Lord's Christ. And he came in the Spirit into the temple, and when the parents brought in the child Jesus, to do for him according to the custom of the Law, he took him up in his arms and blessed God and said, "

"Lord, now you are letting your servant depart in peace, according to your word; for my eyes have seen your salvation that you have prepared in the presence of all peoples, a light for revelation to the Gentiles, and for glory to your people Israel."
— *Luke 2:25-32 (ESV)*

Simeon received this by faith after the Holy Spirit revealed to him that this child was, indeed, the Messiah, the Savior of the world, that he was so eagerly awaiting. His heart was ready and earnestly seeking Jesus. God will reveal Jesus to you also, if you have an open heart and respond to the Holy Spirit's tugging on your heart. Do you have an open heart or a closed heart?

Here is a verse that shows how Jesus builds faith in John, the Baptist by His words when John was in prison for his faith.

"Now when John heard in prison about the deeds of the Christ, he sent word by his disciples and said to him, "Are you the one who is to come, or shall we look for another?"

And Jesus answered them, "Go and tell John what you hear and see: the blind receive their sight and the lame walk, lepers are cleansed and the deaf hear, and the dead are raised up, and the poor have good news preached to them. And blessed is the one who is not offended by me."
— *Matthew 11:2-6 (ESV)*

John knew Jesus. He had seen the Holy Spirit descend upon Him. Maybe John, being in prison, needed a boost in faith and needed to hear the words of Jesus. Jesus responded – to fill John's heart with faith! John truly believed.

In the following passage, Jesus proclaims to the high priest that He is truly the Christ, the Son of God - but it falls on faithless deaf ears! We all have to make choices when confronted with the truth. Allow God's Word to build faith in your heart. So many people choose to keep "the veil" over their heart and eyes!

"Now the chief priests and the whole council were seeking false testimony against Jesus that they might put him to death, but they found none, though many false witnesses came forward. At last two came forward and said, "This man said, 'I am able to destroy the temple of God, and to rebuild it in three days.'"

And the high priest stood up and said, "Have you no answer to make? What is it that these men testify against you?"

But Jesus remained silent. And the high priest said to him, "I adjure you by the living God, tell us if you are the Christ, the Son of God."

Jesus said to him, "You have said so. But I tell you, from now on you will see the Son of Man seated at the right hand of Power and coming on the clouds of heaven."
— Matthew 26:59-64 (ESV)

"You search the Scriptures because you think that in them you have eternal life; and it is they that bear witness about me, yet you refuse to come to me that you may have life."
— John 5:39-40 (ESV)

Messiah, Redeemer, and Savior

Similarly, when Peter reveals the truth to the religious rulers
- after Jesus' death and resurrection - they too had to make a
choice - to believe or not believe? Sadly, very very few did
believe and follow Jesus, but the majority did not obey the
Gospel that they may believe and be saved. They remained
in their sins.

*"But Peter and the apostles answered, "We must obey God
rather than men. The God of our fathers raised Jesus, whom
you killed by hanging him on a tree. God exalted him at his
right hand as Leader and Savior, to give repentance to Israel
and forgiveness of sins. And we are witnesses to these things,
and so is the Holy Spirit, whom God has given to those who
obey him."*
— *Acts 5:29-32 (ESV)*

Here is the gospel truth - what will we do with it?

*"For all have sinned and fall short of the glory of God, and are
justified by his grace as a gift, through the redemption that is
in Christ Jesus, whom God put forward as a propitiation by
his blood, to be received by faith. This was to show God's
righteousness, because in his divine forbearance he had passed
over former sins. It was to show his righteousness at the
present time, so that he might be just and the justifier of the
one who has faith in Jesus."*
— *Romans 3:23-26 (ESV)*

Our God is so full of mercy and grace. He did the ultimate to
save us. Not only did He pay the price, but, He lovingly sends
His Holy Spirit to do the eternal "work" in our hearts when

48

we reach out to Him in our weakness. Faith is a gift. He freely gives us this gift when we truly open our hearts to Him. **How great is our God!**

"But what does it say? "The word is near you, in your mouth and in your heart" (that is, the word of faith that we proclaim); because, if you confess with your mouth that Jesus is Lord and believe in your heart that God raised him from the dead, you will be saved. For with the heart one believes and is justified, and with the mouth one confesses and is saved. For the Scripture says, "Everyone who believes in him will not be put to shame." For there is no distinction between Jew and Greek; for the same Lord is Lord of all, bestowing his riches on all who call on him. For "everyone who calls on the name of the Lord will be saved."
— *Romans 10:8-13 (ESV)*

"If we receive the testimony of men, the testimony of God is greater, for this is the testimony of God that he has borne concerning his Son. Whoever believes in the Son of God has the testimony in himself. Whoever does not believe God has made him a liar, because he has not believed in the testimony that God has borne concerning his Son.

And this is the testimony, that God gave us eternal life, and this life is in his Son. Whoever has the Son has life; whoever does not have the Son of God does not have life.

I write these things to you who believe in the name of the Son of God, that you may know that you have eternal life."
— *1 John 5:9-13 (ESV)*

Messiah, Redeemer, and Savior

Nothing will give you more inner peace and *true tranquility* than to **know** you have eternal life, to know that Jesus – the God of the universe – loves you and actually lives in your heart. God's Word also says that He "inhabits" the prayers and praises of His saints. Everyone who has truly placed their faith and trust in Him is one of His saints. **True inner peace and tranquility is only found in Jesus.**

CHAPTER 10

The Risen One

The very core of Christian faith and the undeniable truth on which we stand is that **Jesus *rose from the dead*.** The Resurrection of Jesus, three days after He died on the cross and was buried, is essential to the saving of our souls. It is the very heart of our faith.

In the last topic, we found in Romans:

"But what does it say? "The word is near you, in your mouth and in your heart" (that is, the word of faith that we proclaim); because, if you confess with your mouth that Jesus is Lord and believe in your heart that God raised him from the dead, you will be saved. For with the heart one believes and is justified, and with the mouth one confesses and is saved."
— Romans 10:8-10 (ESV)

The Risen One

Paul confirmed this again in his letter to the Corinthians.

"For I delivered to you as of first importance what I also received: that Christ died for our sins in accordance with the Scriptures, that he was buried, that he was raised on the third day in accordance with the Scriptures, and that he appeared to Cephas, then to the twelve. Then he appeared to more than five hundred brothers at one time, most of whom are still alive, though some have fallen asleep. Then he appeared to James, then to all the apostles. Last of all, as to one untimely born, he appeared also to me. For I am the least of the apostles, unworthy to be called an apostle, because I persecuted the church of God."
— *1 Corinthians 15:3-9 (ESV)*

Please stop and read the last two Scriptures again!

Now I have a question for you: What are the first reactions or feelings that you find rising up in your heart when you read these Scriptures? It is a very important question.

One reaction might be **indifference** – you don't really know for sure and you don't really care. Another reaction might be **skepticism** – *"Are you serious? What a big fairy tale! Do you really believe that nonsense?"* Another reaction is **one of true joy** and a **knowing** in your heart that Jesus is alive and well.

True born-again believing children of God, when reading or hearing Scriptures such as these, sense a firm, joyful affirmation in their heart that indeed, their Savior is risen and that He is truly coming back again – just as He promised.

There is, however, a fourth reaction – that of Christians who for whatever reason are not walking in fellowship with their Lord. They are backslidden, living in sin. They are not living in a manner that is pleasing to their Lord and Savior. Their reaction would be one of – *sadness and maybe even fear.* There is definitely an affirmation in their heart that Jesus truly rose from the dead, but their joy is gone because they know they are not right with their God. *To you, my brother or sister, I say, "Come back to your Lord – He loves you so much! Why would you want to stay away and out of fellowship with a God who loves and adores you so much?"*

You who have a reaction of indifference or a mocking attitude have definitely **not** been reborn by the Spirit of God. *You are still lost in your sins.* When someone cries out to God in faith, wanting to really know the truth, willing to repent and trust Jesus as Savior and Lord – *a miracle truly happens!* The Spirit of God imparts to that person the **"gift of faith"**! The Holy Spirit makes it possible for the "heart" of that man, woman, or child to *truly believe* and have that **"knowing"** in their heart. They are **born-again.**

"For by grace you have been saved through faith. And this is not your own doing; it is the gift of God, not a result of works, so that no one may boast. For we are his workmanship, created in Christ Jesus for good works, which God prepared beforehand, that we should walk in them."
— *Ephesians 2:8-10 (ESV)*

My friend, if you are one who does not have that joyful affirmation, but instead feels indifference or even a mocking attitude, *please do not throw this book aside and walk away.* Please give yourself the rest of this hour or so to at least search this out. Keep reading, please.

Father, in the name of Jesus, I pray now for this friend, that as he or she searches this out You will flood their heart with Your light and reveal Your Son, Jesus! Please grant Your amazing gift of saving faith! Amen!

Read on, my friend.

After Jesus rose from the dead, He appeared to many, including the disciples – however, Thomas was not with them. When they told Thomas that they had seen Jesus, he wouldn't believe them. Thomas' was faithless.

"So the other disciples told him, "We have seen the Lord." But he said to them, "Unless I see in his hands the mark of the nails, and place my finger into the mark of the nails, and place my hand into his side, I will never believe."
— John 20:25 (ESV)

But, Jesus, in His mercy and compassion, pursued Thomas.

"Eight days later, his disciples were inside again, and Thomas was with them. Although the doors were locked, Jesus came and stood among them and said, "Peace be with you." Then he said to Thomas, "Put your finger here, and see my hands; and put out your hand, and place it in my side. Do not disbelieve, but believe." Thomas answered him, "My Lord and my God!" Jesus said to him, "Have you believed because you have seen me? Blessed are those who have not seen and

yet have believed." Now Jesus did many other signs in the presence of the disciples, which are not written in this book; but these are written so that you may believe that Jesus is the Christ, the Son of God, and that by believing you may have life in his name."
— *John 20:26-31 (ESV)*

Because faith comes by hearing the Word of God – the Good News of Jesus – here are a number of Scriptures that will continue to build faith within your heart.

Matthew, Mark, Luke, and John – the writers of the four Gospels of the New Testament, were all witnesses of Jesus' life, His death, and His resurrection. They all saw Him after He rose from the dead. They all give an account of this in their respective Gospels.

"From that time Jesus began to show his disciples that he must go to Jerusalem and suffer many things from the elders and chief priests and scribes, and be killed, and on the third day be raised."
— *Matthew 16:21 (ESV)*

"As they were gathering in Galilee, Jesus said to them, "The Son of Man is about to be delivered into the hands of men, and they will kill him, and he will be raised on the third day." And they were greatly distressed."
— *Matthew 17:22-23 (ESV)*

"And as Jesus was going up to Jerusalem, he took the twelve disciples aside, and on the way he said to them, "See, we are

going up to Jerusalem. And the Son of Man will be delivered over to the chief priests and scribes, and they will condemn him to death and deliver him over to the Gentiles to be mocked and flogged and crucified, and he will be raised on the third day."
— *Matthew 20:17-19 (ESV)*

In these verses Jesus predicted what was going to happen. In the next passage of Scripture – after Jesus died and was buried – is the fulfillment of the promise that Jesus gave them.

"Now after the Sabbath, toward the dawn of the first day of the week, Mary Magdalene and the other Mary went to see the tomb.

And behold, there was a great earthquake, for an angel of the Lord descended from heaven and came and rolled back the stone and sat on it. His appearance was like lightning, and his clothing white as snow. And for fear of him the guards trembled and became like dead men.

But the angel said to the women, "Do not be afraid, for I know that you seek Jesus who was crucified. He is not here, for he has risen, as he said. Come, see the place where he lay. Then go quickly and tell his disciples that he has risen from the dead, and behold, he is going before you to Galilee; there you will see him. See, I have told you."

So they departed quickly from the tomb with fear and great joy, and ran to tell his disciples. And behold, Jesus met them and said, "Greetings!" And they came up and took hold of his feet and worshiped him.

Then Jesus said to them, "Do not be afraid; go and tell my brothers to go to Galilee, and there they will see me."
— *Matthew 28:1-10 (ESV)*

In Mark's Gospel account:

"And he began to teach them that the Son of Man must suffer many things and be rejected by the elders and the chief priests and the scribes and be killed, and after three days rise again. And he said this plainly. And Peter took him aside and began to rebuke him.

But turning and seeing his disciples, he rebuked Peter and said, "Get behind me, Satan! For you are not setting your mind on the things of God, but on the things of man."
— *Mark 8:31-33 (ESV)*

In Luke's Gospel account:

"And taking the twelve, he said to them, "See, we are going up to Jerusalem, and everything that is written about the Son of Man by the prophets will be accomplished. For he will be delivered over to the Gentiles and will be mocked and shamefully treated and spit upon. And after flogging him, they will kill him, and on the third day he will rise." But they understood none of these things. This saying was hidden from them, and they did not grasp what was said."
— *Luke 18:31-34 (ESV)*

The Risen One

In John's Gospel account the promise fulfilled:

"Now on the first day of the week Mary Magdalene came to the tomb early, while it was still dark, and saw that the stone had been taken away from the tomb. So she ran and went to Simon Peter and the other disciple, the one whom Jesus loved, and said to them, "They have taken the Lord out of the tomb, and we do not know where they have laid him."

So Peter went out with the other disciple, and they were going toward the tomb. Both of them were running together, but the other disciple outran Peter and reached the tomb first. And stooping to look in, he saw the linen cloths lying there, but he did not go in. Then Simon Peter came, following him, and went into the tomb. He saw the linen cloths lying there, and the face cloth, which had been on Jesus' head, not lying with the linen cloths but folded up in a place by itself. Then the other disciple, who had reached the tomb first, also went in, and he saw and believed; for as yet they did not understand the Scripture, that he must rise from the dead. Then the disciples went back to their homes.

But Mary stood weeping outside the tomb, and as she wept she stooped to look into the tomb.

And she saw two angels in white, sitting where the body of Jesus had lain, one at the head and one at the feet. They said to her, "Woman, why are you weeping?" She said to them, "They have taken away my Lord, and I do not know where they have laid him."

Having said this, she turned around and saw Jesus standing, but she did not know that it was Jesus. Jesus said to her, "Woman, why are you weeping? Whom are you seeking?" Supposing him to be the gardener, she said to him, "Sir, if you have carried him away, tell me where you have laid him, and I will take him away." Jesus said to her, "Mary." She turned and said to him in Aramaic, "Rabboni!" (which means Teacher). Jesus said to her, "Do not cling to me, for I have not yet ascended to the Father; but go to my brothers and say to them, 'I am ascending to my Father and your Father, to my God and your God.'"

Mary Magdalene went and announced to the disciples, "I have seen the Lord"—and that he had said these things to her."
— John 20:1-18 (ESV)

Luke, writer of the Book of Acts, had this to say about the 40 days after Jesus rose from the dead:

In my first book I told you, Theophilus, about everything Jesus began to do and teach until the day He was taken up to heaven after giving His chosen apostles further instructions through the Holy Spirit. During the forty days after His crucifixion, He appeared to the apostles from time to time, and He proved to them in many ways that He was actually alive. And He talked to them about the Kingdom of God.

Once He was eating with them, He commanded them, "Do not leave Jerusalem until the Father sends you the gift He

The Risen One

*promised, as I told you before. John baptized with water, but
in just a few days you will be baptized with the Holy Spirit."*
— Acts 1:1-4 (NLT)

Later in the book of Acts, Peter proclaimed this truth to the
Gentiles about the risen Savior:

*"And we apostles are witnesses of all He did throughout Judea
and in Jerusalem. They put Him to death by hanging Him on
a cross, but God raised Him to life on the third day. Then God
allowed Him to appear, not to the general public, but to us
whom God had chosen in advance to be His witnesses. We
were those who ate and drank with Him after He rose from
the dead! And He ordered us to preach everywhere and to
testify that Jesus is the One appointed by God to be the judge
of all – the living and the dead. He is the One all the prophets
testified about, saying that everyone who believes in Him will
have their sins forgiven through His name!"*
— Acts 10:39-43 (NLT)

And the last testimony I want to share with you is from Jesus
Himself. The apostle John wrote the Book of Revelation – **the
amazing Revelation of the end times and what is to be** –
given to John to write down **by Jesus Himself.**

*"The Revelation of Jesus Christ, which God gave Him to show
to His bond-servants, the things which must soon take place;
and He sent and communicated it by His angel to His bond-
servant John, who testified to the word of God and to the
testimony of Jesus Christ, even to all that he saw.*

Blessed is he who reads and those who hear the words of the prophecy, and heed the things which are written in it; for the time is near.

John to the seven churches that are in Asia: Grace to you and peace, from Him who is and who was and who is to come, and from the seven Spirits who are before His throne, and from Jesus Christ, the faithful witness, the firstborn of the dead, and the ruler of the kings of the earth.

To Him who loves us and released us from our sins by His blood— and He has made us to be a kingdom, priests to His God and Father—to Him be the glory and the dominion forever and ever. Amen.

Behold, He is coming with the clouds, and every eye will see Him, even those who pierced Him; and all the tribes of the earth will mourn over Him. So it is to be. Amen. "I am the Alpha and the Omega," says the Lord God, "who is and who was and who is to come, the Almighty."
— Revelation 1:1-8 (NASB)

My friend, I pray that as you have been reading these accounts and the Word of a true and loving Savior, that faith is coming alive in your heart. Ask God to help you understand the Scriptures and that they will transform your heart. It is a pretty sure thing that if you have come this far in this **appeal,** that God is calling you, tugging at your heart, and offering you His wonderful salvation. He loves you so much! Humble yourself before Him – confess to Him that you are a sinner and ask Him to forgive you of all your sins, to save you, and to transform you by His Spirit. Confess out

The Risen One

of your mouth that Jesus is Lord and that you believe in your heart that God has raised Him from the dead.

"For "Whoever will call on the name of the Lord will be saved."
— *Romans 10:13 (NASB)*

"If we confess our sins, He is faithful and righteous to forgive us our sins and to cleanse us from all unrighteousness."
— *1 John 1:9 (NASB)*

Call out to Him, in faith – He **will** hear you.

CHAPTER 11

God of Forgiveness

The compassionate, merciful, and freely forgiving heart of God was most vividly displayed when Jesus, our Lord and Savior, hung on the cross. Racked with pain, whipped, flesh-torn and beaten beyond recognition, pierced through His hands and His feet, a crown of sharp jagged thorns crushed into His skull – the full weight of every sin ever committed by every man, woman, and child since Adam and Eve – laid heavily upon His shoulders. Mocked, spit upon, humiliated and despised – He was truly a man of sorrows.

Then, the Father's face turned away from Him because He could not look upon all of this sin. Instead, the full fury of God's wrath was poured out on Jesus – for our sins. The physical pain, though excruciating, paled in comparison to the spiritual separation that He experienced from the Father.

While enduring the most excruciating pain – physically and spiritually combined – ever experienced by any man, He uttered these words – "***Father, forgive them – for they don't know what they are doing.***" Hardly the words of a harsh, tyrannical, and cruel God as some make Him out, or think Him to be. ***Our God is a merciful, compassionate, forgiving, and loving God.***

Then, immediately after Jesus uttered those words, He was mocked even more. The two criminals hanging on either side of Him, then spoke out and made the **final decision** that they would ever have opportunity to make.

"And the people stood by, looking on. And even the rulers were sneering at Him, saying, "He saved others; let Him save Himself if this is the Christ of God, His Chosen One." The soldiers also mocked Him, coming up to Him, offering Him sour wine, and saying, "If You are the King of the Jews, save Yourself!" Now there was also an inscription above Him, "THIS IS THE KING OF THE JEWS."

One of the criminals who were hanged there was hurling abuse at Him, saying, "Are You not the Christ? Save Yourself and us!"

But the other answered, and rebuking him said, "Do you not even fear God, since you are under the same sentence of condemnation? And we indeed are suffering justly, for we are receiving what we deserve for our deeds; but this man has done nothing wrong."

And he was saying, "Jesus, remember me when You come in Your kingdom!" And He said to him, "Truly I say to you, today you shall be with Me in Paradise."
— *Luke 23:35-43 (NASB)*

What an absolutely beautiful picture of God's love, mercy, grace, and forgiveness. The Holy Spirit draws even lifelong criminals to true repentance. This man allowed the Holy Spirit to flood his heart with light. He acknowledged his sin and he cried out to Jesus to save him. Right before his death, he is **touched by the Savior** and **born again by the Spirit of God.** That, my friend, is true mercy and grace.

But, what about the other criminal? God certainly does not want **anyone** to die in their sin; He wants **everyone** to come to true repentance. This man, however, was not open to the conviction of God's Spirit. He had the same chance as the other criminal, **but he chose to reject his one and only Savior.** The same is true for everyone. So, why do some people open their heart to Jesus and the work of the Holy Spirit, while others stiff-arm Him, reject Him, and walk away from their only Savior?

Do you have an open heart? All the Holy Spirit needs to complete His work of **amazing grace** in you, is your open heart – and your desire to know and cling to the only real truth – Jesus.

CHAPTER 12

Our Conquering King

"Then, when our dying bodies have been transformed into bodies that will never die, the Scripture will be fulfilled: "Death is swallowed up in victory! O death, where is your sting? O grave, where is your victory?"
— *I Corinthians 15: 54-55 (NLT)*

Have you ever wondered why death – especially the death of our closest loved ones – is so incredibly painful and so extremely hard for our human mind, heart, and psyche to process? The grieving process is, for almost everyone, the most painful experience we face. The pain we experience is so deep and so intense, our breath is all but taken from us. Our hearts are shattered. It's as if we are trapped in another world – a world so unreal, so unfair, so dark and painful. We don't know how to make this pain disappear – we feel devastated and many times we feel frighteningly alone.

Everyone goes through different degrees of grieving, but none is exempt from pain.

The reason? ***Death is an unnatural enemy that was never meant to be.*** God never intended for us to die. When He created man and woman, He created us to live forever in fellowship with Him – enjoying Him and walking with Him in the "cool of the day". ***But*** when sin entered the world, death also entered, along with all the evil and pain that goes with it. However, Jesus defeated death on the cross. Sin and death (and all the unnatural things that come with them) will come to an end for all eternity when He returns.

"For Christ must reign until He humbles all His enemies beneath His feet. And the last enemy to be destroyed is death!"
—1 Corinthians 15:25-26 (NLT)

So, when did sin, death and all their unnatural side effects enter our world? The story of creation and the first man and woman – Adam and Eve – tell the whole story.

"Then the Lord God formed man of dust from the ground, and breathed into his nostrils the breath of life; and man became a living being.

The Lord God planted a garden toward the east, in Eden; and there He placed the man whom He had formed. Out of the ground the Lord God caused to grow every tree that is pleasing to the sight and good for food; the tree of life also in the midst of the garden, and the tree of the knowledge of good and evil."
— Genesis 2:7-9 (NASB)

"Then the Lord God took the man and put him into the garden of Eden to cultivate it and keep it. The Lord God commanded the man, saying, "From any tree of the garden you may eat freely; but from the tree of the knowledge of good and evil you shall not eat, for in the day that you eat from it you will surely die."
— *Genesis 2:15-17 (NASB)*

"Then the Lord God said, "It is not good for the man to be alone; I will make him a helper suitable for him."
— *Genesis 2:18 (NASB)*

"So the Lord God caused a deep sleep to fall upon the man, and he slept; then He took one of his ribs and closed up the flesh at that place. The Lord God fashioned into a woman the rib which He had taken from the man, and brought her to the man.

The man said, "This is now bone of my bones, And flesh of my flesh; She shall be called Woman, Because she was taken out of Man."

For this reason a man shall leave his father and his mother, and be joined to his wife; and they shall become one flesh.

And the man and his wife were both naked and were not ashamed."
— *Genesis 2:21-25 (NASB)*

"Now the serpent was more crafty than any beast of the field which the Lord God had made. And he said to the woman,

"Indeed, has God said, 'You shall not eat from any tree of the garden'?"

The woman said to the serpent, "From the fruit of the trees of the garden we may eat; but from the fruit of the tree which is in the middle of the garden, God has said, 'You shall not eat from it or touch it, or you will die."

The serpent said to the woman, "You surely will not die! For God knows that in the day you eat from it your eyes will be opened, and you will be like God, knowing good and evil."

When the woman saw that the tree was good for food, and that it was a delight to the eyes, and that the tree was desirable to make one wise, she took from its fruit and ate; and she gave also to her husband with her, and he ate.

Then the eyes of both of them were opened, and they knew that they were naked; and they sewed fig leaves together and made themselves loin coverings."
— Genesis 3:1-7 (NASB)

That was the fateful moment that sin, death, sickness and every evil side effect entered our world. Until that moment, there was no sin, no pain or sickness, no death, no hatred and jealousy, no aging or deterioration, and on, and on, and on. Sin had destroyed the fellowship and perfect relationship between man and his God and – the world around him. When God told Adam that the day he ate of that fruit he would surely die, He wasn't referring to an instantaneous death – He was referring to the death process. That process has affected every person who has ever been born since.

"They heard the sound of the Lord God walking in the garden in the cool of the day, and the man and his wife hid themselves from the presence of the Lord God among the trees of the garden. Then the Lord God called to the man, and said to him, "Where are you?"

He said, "I heard the sound of You in the garden, and I was afraid because I was naked; so I hid myself."

And He said, "Who told you that you were naked? Have you eaten from the tree of which I commanded you not to eat?"
— Genesis 3:8-11 (NASB)

You can read the whole heart-breaking account in Genesis chapters 2 & 3. You will see that, after God made known to Adam and Eve all the unnatural life-altering changes and patterns that would transpire because of their sin, He would have to banish them from the Garden of Eden.

The reason He could not let them stay in the Garden of Eden was that if they had eaten the fruit from the Tree of Life *after* they had sinned, all mankind would have lived forever in their horrible sinful state – **never again to be right with their Creator.** God would not have been able to redeem man through the death and blood of Jesus. This unnatural enemy – death – had to remain – at least for now.

"Then the Lord God said, "Behold, the man has become like one of Us, knowing good and evil; and now, he might stretch out his hand, and take also from the tree of life, and eat, and live forever"— therefore the Lord God sent him out from the

garden of Eden, to cultivate the ground from which he was taken.

So He drove the man out; and at the east of the garden of Eden He stationed the cherubim and the flaming sword which turned every direction to guard the way to the tree of life."
— *Genesis 3:22-24 (NASB)*

Ever since that time, God has been in the process of redeeming man back to Himself. God's Word, the Bible, is the complete story of the **redemption and salvation** that God, through Jesus Christ, made possible and readily available to every man, woman, and child – throughout all generations. When you get to the end of God's book, the Bible – you will discover that Jesus is absolutely, without a doubt the Redeemer to **all** who place their trust and faith in Him and **Him only. Jesus is our Conquering King.**

Revelation, the final book of the Bible, is a prophecy given to John from Jesus himself. It gives a vivid description of what will be and what will soon take place. Every person alive should read this whole revelation. Here is just a very small portion of His Revelation – showing that Jesus is, indeed, the King of kings.

"And I saw heaven opened, and behold, a white horse, and He who sat on it is called Faithful and True, and in righteousness He judges and wages war. His eyes are a flame of fire, and on His head are many diadems; and He has a name written on Him which no one knows except Himself. He is clothed with a robe dipped in blood, and His name is called The Word of God.

And the armies which are in heaven, clothed in fine linen, white and clean, were following Him on white horses. From His mouth comes a sharp sword, so that with it He may strike down the nations, and He will rule them with a rod of iron; and He treads the wine press of the fierce wrath of God, the Almighty. And on His robe and on His thigh He has a name written, "KING OF KINGS, AND LORD OF LORDS."
— *Revelation 19:11-16 (NASB)*

My friend, you will, most assuredly, want to be on the side of our Conquering King. Give your heart to Him today. He loves you and you can trust Him completely – with your very life.

CHAPTER 13

Our Soon Coming King

Another core and foundational truth of our Christian faith is the **Second Coming of Jesus** – to this earth. Just like His death, burial, and resurrection, believing in His Second Coming is also essential to the saving of our souls. There were many, many prophecies all through the Old Testament foretelling the Advent or First Coming of Jesus – His birth, life, death, and His resurrection. They all, without fail, came to pass. There are many more prophecies in the Old *and* New Testaments of our Savior's Second Coming. They also, without fail, will come to pass. Every true born again believing child of God has that *"knowing"* in their heart. They have that firm, joyful affirmation – our Blessed Hope – our Blessed Assurance.

In the book of Acts – after the forty day period when Jesus appeared to more than 500 people and affirmed that He truly *arose from the dead*, He told them many things that would come to be and then He *ascended into heaven* – right before their very eyes. Here is the account of this awesome event.

So when the apostles were with Jesus, they kept asking Him, "Lord, has the time come for you to free Israel and restore our kingdom?"

He replied, "The Father alone has the authority to set those dates and times, and they are not for you to know. But, you will receive power when the Holy Spirit comes upon you. And you will be My witnesses, telling people about Me everywhere – in Jerusalem, throughout Judea, in Samaria, and to the ends of the earth."

After saying this, He was taken up into a cloud, while they were watching, and they could no longer see Him. As they strained to see Him rising into heaven, two white-robed men suddenly stood among them. "Men of Galilee", they said, "why are you standing here staring into heaven? Jesus has been taken from you into heaven, but someday He will return from heaven in the same way you saw Him go!"
— *Acts 1:6-9 (NLT)*

You may have heard of an event that is known as the "Rapture". It is the "catching away" of all the born-again believers who are living on earth when Jesus comes back - to meet us in the air. The Rapture is actually an event before His Second Coming. The 7 year Tribulation period starts right after the Rapture and culminates at His Second Coming, when we return with Jesus to this earth to set up His Millennial Kingdom on this earth for a 1000 years. Paul describes the Rapture in his book to the Thessalonians.

"And now dear brothers and sisters, we want you to know what will happen to the believers who have died - so you will not grieve as people who have no hope. For since we believe that Jesus died and was raised to life again, we also believe that when Jesus returns, God will bring back with Him the believers who have died. We tell you this directly from the Lord: We who are still living when the Lord returns will not meet Him ahead of those who have died. For the Lord Himself will come down from heaven with a commanding shout, with the voice of the archangel, and with the trumpet call of God. First, the Christians who have died will rise from their graves. Then, together with them, we who are still alive and remain on the earth will be "caught up" in the clouds to meet the Lord in the air. Then, we will be with the Lord forever!"
— *1 Thessalonians 4:13-18 (NLT)*

Paul also describes it in his letter to the Corinthians. You can read the whole 15th chapter of I Corinthians – but here is a portion of the chapter.

But let me reveal to you a wonderful secret. We will not all die, but we will all be transformed. It will happen in a moment, in the blink of an eye, when the last trumpet is blown. For when the trumpet sounds, those who have died will be raised to live forever. And we who are living will also be transformed. For our dying bodies must be transformed into bodies that will never die; our mortal bodies must be transformed into immortal bodies.

Then when our dying bodies have been transformed into bodies that will never die, this Scripture will be fulfilled:

77

"Death is swallowed up in victory! O death, where is your sting? O grave, where is your victory?

For sin is the sting that results in death, and the law gives sin its power. BUT, thank God! He gives us the victory over sin and death through our Lord Jesus Christ.

So, my dear brothers and sisters, be strong and immovable. Always work enthusiastically for the Lord, for you know that nothing you do for the Lord is ever useless!
— 1 Corinthians 15:51-58 (NLT)

Now, I want to give you the Words of Jesus himself – given from a God who cannot lie.

"Then if anyone tells you, 'Look, here is the Messiah,' or 'There He is,' don't believe it. For false messiahs and false prophets will rise up and perform great signs and wonders so as to deceive, if possible, even God's chosen ones! See, I have warned you about this ahead of time.

So, if someone tells you, 'Look the Messiah is out in the desert,' don't bother to go and look. Or, 'Look He is hiding here,' don't believe it. For as the lightening flashes in the east and shines to the west, so it will be when the Son of Man comes. Just as the gathering of vultures shows there is a carcass nearby, so these signs indicate that the end is near.

Immediately after the anguish of those days, the sun will be darkened, the moon will give no light, the stars will fall from the sky, and the powers in the heaven will be shaken.

And then at last, the sign that the Son of Man is coming will appear in the heavens, and there will be deep mourning among all the peoples of the earth. And they will see the Son of Man coming on the clouds of heaven with power and great glory! And He will send out His angels with the mighty blast of a trumpet, and they will gather His chosen ones from all over the world – from the farthest ends of the earth and heaven.

Now learn a lesson from the fig tree. When its branches bud and its leaves begin to sprout, you know that summer is near. In the same way, when you see all these things, you can know His return is very near, right at the door. I tell you the truth, that generation will not pass from the scene until all these things take place. Heaven and earth will disappear, but My words will never disappear!

However, no one knows the day or hour when these things will happen, not even the angels in heaven or the Son Himself. Only the Father knows!

When the Son of Man returns, it will be like it was in Noah's day. In those days before the flood, the people were enjoying banquets and parties and weddings right up to the time Noah entered his boat. People didn't realize what was going to happen until the flood came and swept them all away. That is the way it will be when the Son of Man comes.

Two men will be working together in the field; one will be taken, the other left. Two women will be grinding flour at the mill; one will be taken, the other left.

So, you too, must keep watch. For you don't know what day your Lord is coming!"
— *Matthew 24:23-31 (NLT)*

There are many more Scriptures that explain and foretell the Second Coming of Jesus. To those people who have not allowed the Holy Spirit to enlighten them and to "flood their heart with His light", these promises will all seem like nothing but fairy tales – nonsense. Or, they just won't care at all. Many people will mock it and laugh about such things. But, just as Jesus reminded us, in the days of Noah, many people – the overwhelming majority – mocked and ridiculed Noah until the day the flood began. So, instead of being "flooded with His light" – they were flooded with water. That was not intended to be funny in any way – very sad, actually.

So shall it be when Jesus comes back. Those who refuse to believe, repent, and place their faith and trust in Jesus will suddenly be overwhelmed. All hope will be lost – forever.

To those who are searching and ***want to believe*** – but just aren't quite sure – please ask God to give you the faith you need to believe. He knows your heart – He knows everything about you. Seek and you will find. Ask and it will be given. God absolutely loves and honors a heart that seeks Him. Remember – faith is a gift of God – given to those who truly seek and ask.

CHAPTER 14

The Restoration of All Things

In this *appeal*, I'm sure that you have noticed all of the many names and titles that Jesus adorns. He is our everything. He is worthy of all of our worship, all of our praise, and all of our hearts. Another title that He will acquire from His Second Coming throughout all eternity is – the *"Restoration of All Things"*. Jesus will make all things new. Even our bodies will be made new – *glorified* - without flaw, without pain and disease, without death, and without tears – for He will wipe every tear from our eyes. What a joyful and beautiful picture of our future reality – a reality that He has set before us. Let us run this race, looking through the eye of faith - keeping our eyes on Jesus, the author and finisher of our faith.

The Restoration of All Things

Before Jesus makes all things new, He shall destroy all the works of the devil, of sin and of death. As we saw in the last topic that the last enemy that will be destroyed is death. Jesus will right every wrong.

"For after all it is only just for God to repay with affliction those who afflict you, and to give relief to you who are afflicted and to us as well when the Lord Jesus will be revealed from heaven with His mighty angels in flaming fire, dealing out retribution to those who do not know God and to those who do not obey the gospel of our Lord Jesus. These will pay the penalty of eternal destruction, away from the presence of the Lord and from the glory of His power, when He comes to be glorified in His saints on that day, and to be marveled at among all who have believed—for our testimony to you was believed."
— *11 Thessalonians 1:6-10 (NASB)*

"Now we request you, brethren, with regard to the coming of our Lord Jesus Christ and our gathering together to Him, that you not be quickly shaken from your composure or be disturbed either by a spirit or a message or a letter as if from us, to the effect that the day of the Lord has come.

Let no one in any way deceive you, for it will not come unless the apostasy comes first, and the man of lawlessness is revealed, the son of destruction, who opposes and exalts himself above every so-called god or object of worship, so that he takes his seat in the temple of God, displaying himself as being God.

82

Do you not remember that while I was still with you, I was telling you these things? And you know what restrains him now, so that in his time he will be revealed. For the mystery of lawlessness is already at work; only he who now restrains will do so until he is taken out of the way.

Then that lawless one will be revealed whom the Lord will slay with the breath of His mouth and bring to an end by the appearance of His coming; that is, the one whose coming is in accord with the activity of Satan, with all power and signs and false wonders, and with all the deception of wickedness for those who perish, because they did not receive the love of the truth so as to be saved.

For this reason God will send upon them a deluding influence so that they will believe what is false, in order that they all may be judged who did not believe the truth, but took pleasure in wickedness."
— *11 Thessalonians 2:1-12 (NASB)*

<u>The final defeat of the beast and false prophet</u> as recorded in Revelation:

"Then I saw an angel standing in the sun, and he cried out with a loud voice, saying to all the birds which fly in midheaven, "Come, assemble for the great supper of God, so that you may eat the flesh of kings and the flesh of commanders and the flesh of mighty men and the flesh of horses and of those who sit on them and the flesh of all men, both free men and slaves, and small and great."

The Restoration of All Things

*And I saw the beast and the kings of the earth and their armies
assembled to make war against Him who sat on the horse and
against His army. And the beast was seized, and with him the
false prophet who performed the signs in his presence, by
which he deceived those who had received the mark of the
beast and those who worshiped his image; these two were
thrown alive into the lake of fire which burns with brimstone.
And the rest were killed with the sword which came from the
mouth of Him who sat on the horse, and all the birds were
filled with their flesh."*
— Revelation 19:17-21 (NASB)

<u>The final defeat of Satan</u> – as recorded in the book of
Revelation. There is much more that happens before his
defeat – you can read it all in Revelation.

*"Then I saw an angel coming down from heaven, holding the
key of the abyss and a great chain in his hand. And he laid
hold of the dragon, the serpent of old, who is the devil and
Satan, and bound him for a thousand years; and he threw him
into the abyss, and shut it and sealed it over him, so that he
would not deceive the nations any longer, until the thousand
years were completed; after these things he must be released
for a short time."*
— Revelation 20:1-3 (NASB)

*"When the thousand years are completed, Satan will be
released from his prison, and will come out to deceive the
nations which are in the four corners of the earth, Gog and
Magog, to gather them together for the war; the number of*

them is like the sand of the seashore. And they came up on the broad plain of the earth and surrounded the camp of the saints and the beloved city, and fire came down from heaven and devoured them. And the devil who deceived them was thrown into the lake of fire and brimstone, where the beast and the false prophet are also; and they will be tormented day and night forever and ever."
— *Revelation 20:7-10 (NASB)*

The **_final judgement_** as recorded in the book of Revelation.

"Then I saw a great white throne and Him who sat upon it, from whose presence earth and heaven fled away, and no place was found for them. And I saw the dead, the great and the small, standing before the throne, and books were opened; and another book was opened, which is the book of life; and the dead were judged from the things which were written in the books, according to their deeds. And the sea gave up the dead which were in it, and death and Hades gave up the dead which were in them; and they were judged, every one of them according to their deeds. Then death and Hades were thrown into the lake of fire. This is the second death, the lake of fire. And if anyone's name was not found written in the book of life, he was thrown into the lake of fire."
— *Revelation 20:11-15 (NASB)*

Now with the devil, sin, and death destroyed and forever gone – Jesus will make all things new! Chapters 21 and 22 of Revelation give the description of what will take place. God reveals what He has planned for his loved ones – His Bride. Enjoy!

The Restoration of All Things

"Then I saw a new heaven and a new earth; for the first heaven and the first earth passed away, and there is no longer any sea. And I saw the holy city, new Jerusalem, coming down out of heaven from God, made ready as a bride adorned for her husband. And I heard a loud voice from the throne, saying, "Behold, the tabernacle of God is among men, and He will dwell among them, and they shall be His people, and God Himself will be among them, and He will wipe away every tear from their eyes; and there will no longer be any death; there will no longer be any mourning, or crying, or pain; the first things have passed away."

And He who sits on the throne said, "Behold, I am making all things new." And He *said, "Write, for these words are faithful and true." Then He said to me, "It is done. I am the Alpha and the Omega, the beginning and the end. I will give to the one who thirsts from the spring of the water of life without cost. He who overcomes will inherit these things, and I will be his God and he will be My son. But for the cowardly and unbelieving and abominable and murderers and immoral persons and sorcerers and idolaters and all liars, their part will be in the lake that burns with fire and brimstone, which is the second death."

Then one of the seven angels who had the seven bowls full of the seven last plagues came and spoke with me, saying, "Come here, I will show you the bride, the wife of the Lamb."

And he carried me away in the Spirit to a great and high mountain, and showed me the holy city, Jerusalem, coming down out of heaven from God, having the glory of God. Her brilliance was like a very costly stone, as a stone of crystal-clear jasper. It had a great and high wall, with twelve gates, and at the gates twelve angels; and names were written on them, which are the names of the twelve tribes of the sons of Israel. There were three gates on the east and three gates on the north and three gates on the south and three gates on the west. And the wall of the city had twelve foundation stones, and on them were the twelve names of the twelve apostles of the Lamb.

The one who spoke with me had a gold measuring rod to measure the city, and its gates and its wall. The city is laid out as a square, and its length is as great as the width; and he measured the city with the rod, fifteen hundred miles; its length and width and height are equal. And he measured its wall, seventy-two yards, according to human measurements, which are also angelic measurements. The material of the wall was jasper; and the city was pure gold, like clear glass. The foundation stones of the city wall were adorned with every kind of precious stone. The first foundation stone was jasper; the second, sapphire; the third, chalcedony; the fourth, emerald; the fifth, sardonyx; the sixth, sardius; the seventh, chrysolite; the eighth, beryl; the ninth, topaz; the tenth, chrysoprase; the eleventh, jacinth; the twelfth, amethyst. And the twelve gates were twelve pearls; each one of the gates was a single pearl. And the street of the city was pure gold, like transparent glass.

I saw no temple in it, for the Lord God the Almighty and the Lamb are its temple. And the city has no need of the sun or of the moon to shine on it, for the glory of God has illumined it,

and its lamp is the Lamb. The nations will walk by its light, and the kings of the earth will bring their glory into it. In the daytime (for there will be no night there) its gates will never be closed; and they will bring the glory and the honor of the nations into it; and nothing unclean, and no one who practices abomination and lying, shall ever come into it, but only those whose names are written in the Lamb's book of life."
— *Revelation 21:1-27 (NASB)*

"Then he showed me a river of the water of life, clear as crystal, coming from the throne of God and of the Lamb, in the middle of its street. On either side of the river was the tree of life, bearing twelve kinds of fruit, yielding its fruit every month; and the leaves of the tree were for the healing of the nations. There will no longer be any curse; and the throne of God and of the Lamb will be in it, and His bond-servants will serve Him; they will see His face, and His name will be on their foreheads. And there will no longer be any night; and they will not have need of the light of a lamp nor the light of the sun, because the Lord God will illumine them; and they will reign forever and ever.

And he said to me, "These words are faithful and true"; and the Lord, the God of the spirits of the prophets, sent His angel to show to His bond-servants the things which must soon take place.

"And behold, I am coming quickly. Blessed is he who heeds the words of the prophecy of this book."

I, John, am the one who heard and saw these things. And when I heard and saw, I fell down to worship at the feet of the angel who showed me these things. But he *said to me, "Do not do that. I am a fellow servant of yours and of your brethren the prophets and of those who heed the words of this book. Worship God."

And he *said to me, "Do not seal up the words of the prophecy of this book, for the time is near. Let the one who does wrong, still do wrong; and the one who is filthy, still be filthy; and let the one who is righteous, still practice righteousness; and the one who is holy, still keep himself holy."

"Behold, I am coming quickly, and My reward is with Me, to render to every man according to what he has done. I am the Alpha and the Omega, the first and the last, the beginning and the end."

Blessed are those who wash their robes, so that they may have the right to the tree of life, and may enter by the gates into the city. Outside are the dogs and the sorcerers and the immoral persons and the murderers and the idolaters, and everyone who loves and practices lying.

"I, Jesus, have sent My angel to testify to you these things for the churches. I am the root and the descendant of David, the bright morning star."

The Spirit and the bride say, "Come." And let the one who hears say, "Come." And let the one who is thirsty come; let the one who wishes take the water of life without cost.

The Restoration of All Things

I testify to everyone who hears the words of the prophecy of this book: if anyone adds to them, God will add to him the plagues which are written in this book; and if anyone takes away from the words of the book of this prophecy, God will take away his part from the tree of life and from the holy city, which are written in this book.

He who testifies to these things says, "Yes, I am coming quickly." Amen. Come, Lord Jesus. The grace of the Lord Jesus be with all. Amen."
— Revelation 22:1-21 (NASB)

I will add nothing more.

CHAPTER 15

....

The Bridegroom

J esus is beautiful. Our God – so beautiful and glorious in holiness. God – the Father, Son, and Holy Spirit – absolutely beautiful. Jesus radiates God's own glory and expresses the very character of God – the very Beauty of our God. (Based on Hebrews 1:3)

The psalmist, David, expresses his main desire in life.

"One thing I have asked from the Lord, that I shall seek: That I may dwell in the house of the Lord all the days of my life, To behold the beauty of the Lord And to meditate in His temple." — *Psalms 27:4 (NASB)*

David is known in God's Word as "the man after God's own heart." What an awesome legacy to acquire and be known for – throughout all of eternity. David is now enjoying his desire. He is dwelling in the house of his Lord – ***forever*** – and he is definitely *beholding His beauty – forever. To be absent from the body is to be present with the Lord. (based on II Corinthians 5:8)*

Yet, another glorious event will be coming soon – just over the horizon. God will be glorified and His Lordship – finally and forever – fully realized and declared – when every knee bows and every tongue confesses that Jesus Christ is Lord, to the glory of God, the Father.

But then – *the beauty of our Lord* – a beauty that has yet to be experienced or seen by any human heart or eye – will be fully manifested at this glorious event. Every true child of God longs for and excitedly looks forward to (and should be preparing for) this event – an event known as the *"Marriage Supper of the Lamb" and the "Wedding Feast of the Lamb". Our Wedding Day! Jesus is the handsome, loving Bridegroom – and we, the body of Christ (all true believers from all generations) – are His glorious bride.*

There has never been, nor will ever be, a wedding as glorious and beautiful as this. Imagine with me, if you will, this Royal Wedding. Think of the most beautiful, exquisite bride, the most handsome Bridegroom, and the absolute finest of everything. Think of the most beautiful flowers, a glorious wedding hall and banquet room, the finest of food and wine, the most beautiful wedding attire, your believing loved ones, the finest music and dancing. This Celebration of All Celebrations will be way beyond all that. Just imagine Jesus – His breathtaking beauty! The full glory of our God displayed for us to enjoy forever! It will be the most beautiful and awesome day of our dreams. Our day to remember. Our Divine Romance.

God gives us glimpses of His beauty and the glorious things we will enjoy with Him, but words and descriptions do not even exist in our human minds and experiences to even come close to explaining the things that God has prepared for His loved ones – us.

"But just as it is written, "Things which eye has not seen and ear has not heard, And which have not entered the heart of man, All that God has prepared for those who love Him."
— *1 Corinthians 2:9 (NASB)*

Oh, may we ready ourselves for that day. We will see our Jesus face to face! We will dine with Him, dance with Him, laugh with Him, and forever enjoy Him! *All things have been made new!*

Here are some of the events leading up to the *"Wedding Feast of the Lamb"* as recorded in Revelation 19. It all starts with a song of victory.

"After these things I heard something like a loud voice of a great multitude in heaven, saying, "Hallelujah! Salvation and glory and power belong to our God; because His judgments are true and righteous; for He has judged the great harlot who was corrupting the earth with her immorality, and He has avenged the blood of His bond-servants on her." And a second time they said, "Hallelujah! Her smoke rises up forever and ever."

And the twenty-four elders and the four living creatures fell down and worshiped God who sits on the throne saying,

The Bridegoom

"Amen. Hallelujah!" And a voice came from the throne, saying, "Give praise to our God, all you His bond-servants, you who fear Him, the small and the great."

Then I heard something like the voice of a great multitude and like the sound of many waters and like the sound of mighty peals of thunder, saying, "Hallelujah! For the Lord our God, the Almighty, reigns. Let us rejoice and be glad and give the glory to Him, for the marriage of the Lamb has come and His bride has made herself ready."

It was given to her to clothe herself in fine linen, bright and clean; for the fine linen is the righteous acts of the saints. Then he *said to me, "Write, 'Blessed are those who are invited to the marriage supper of the Lamb.'" And he *said to me, "These are true words of God."
— Revelation 19:1-9 (NASB)

Psalm 45 is a Psalm of the sons of Korah that gives a beautiful portrayal of the glory of the Son of God – Jesus – our Handsome Bridegroom. It also gives us an idea of His thoughts toward us – His glorious bride.

"My heart overflows with a good theme; I address my verses to the King; My tongue is the pen of a ready writer. You are fairer than the sons of men; Grace is poured upon Your lips; Therefore God has blessed You forever. Gird Your sword on Your thigh, O Mighty One, In Your splendor and Your majesty! And in Your majesty ride on victoriously, For the cause of truth and meekness and righteousness; Let Your right hand teach You awesome things. Your arrows are sharp; The

peoples fall under You; Your arrows are in the heart of the King's enemies. Your throne, O God, is forever and ever; A scepter of uprightness is the scepter of Your kingdom. You have loved righteousness and hated wickedness; Therefore God, Your God, has anointed You With the oil of joy above Your fellows. All Your garments are fragrant with myrrh and aloes and cassia; Out of ivory palaces stringed instruments have made You glad. Kings' daughters are among Your noble ladies; At Your right hand stands the queen in gold from Ophir. Listen, O daughter, give attention and incline your ear: Forget your people and your father's house; Then the King will desire your beauty. Because He is your Lord, bow down to Him. The daughter of Tyre will come with a gift; The rich among the people will seek your favor. The King's daughter is all glorious within; Her clothing is interwoven with gold. She will be led to the King in embroidered work; The virgins, her companions who follow her, Will be brought to You. They will be led forth with gladness and rejoicing; They will enter into the King's palace. In place of your fathers will be your sons; You shall make them princes in all the earth. I will cause Your name to be remembered in all generations; Therefore the peoples will give You thanks forever and ever."
— Psalm 45:1-17 (NASB)

There is nothing and no one as beautiful as our King! Rejoice in Him!

CHAPTER 16

Heaven or Hell?
A Personal Choice

Make no mistake about it - Hell is real! Heaven is real! And yes, Satan and demons do exist! God's Word is extremely clear and goes to great lengths to teach and warn us about these things. Many people make the fatal mistake of thinking that their opinion somehow matters or that these things are all just fairytales and could never really happen to them. Believing anything other than God's Word will ultimately prove to be a fatal mistake.

It may surprise you to know that, in His ministry, Jesus taught more about Hell than He did about Heaven. He was crystal clear about the reality and the horror of Hell. He didn't sugarcoat or mince His words, nor did He avoid the subject altogether, like most people do today. The closest that most people come to talking about Hell, is to joke about it. Granted, it is a very uncomfortable subject, but one that must be addressed. Contrary to popular approach, however, it is no joking matter.

So here are the facts - according to God's Word. God's Word is the only standard that MUST be considered. Our opinions have absolutely no bearing, one way or the other, on the real truth.

"And just as each person is destined to die once and after that comes judgment, so also Christ was offered once for all time as a sacrifice to take away the sins of many people. He will come again, not to deal with our sins, but to bring salvation to all who are eagerly waiting for him."
— Hebrews 9:27-28 (NLT)

When a person dies, their body is buried (or cremated), but their spirit and soul live eternally. They either go to Hell or Heaven. The Bible says that when a believer dies they are absent from the body but are present with the Lord in Heaven - not so with an unbeliever.

"Yes, we are fully confident, and we would rather be away from these earthly bodies, for then we will be at home with the Lord."
— 2 Corinthians 5:8 (NLT)

Jesus told a true story about two men who lived and then died - a rich man and Lazarus. This is a crystal clear picture of what happens when a person dies.

"Jesus said, "There was a certain rich man who was splendidly clothed in purple and fine linen and who lived each day in

luxury. At his gate lay a poor man named Lazarus who was covered with sores. As Lazarus lay there longing for scraps from the rich man's table, the dogs would come and lick his open sores.

"Finally, the poor man died and was carried by the angels to sit beside Abraham at the heavenly banquet. The rich man also died and was buried, and he went to the place of the dead.

There, in torment, he saw Abraham in the far distance with Lazarus at his side. "The rich man shouted, 'Father Abraham, have some pity! Send Lazarus over here to dip the tip of his finger in water and cool my tongue. I am in anguish in these flames.' "But Abraham said to him, 'Son, remember that during your lifetime you had everything you wanted, and Lazarus had nothing. So now he is here being comforted, and you are in anguish. And besides, there is a great chasm separating us. No one can cross over to you from here, and no one can cross over to us from there.'

"Then the rich man said, 'Please, Father Abraham, at least send him to my father's home. For I have five brothers, and I want him to warn them so they don't end up in this place of torment.' "But Abraham said, 'Moses and the prophets have warned them. Your brothers can read what they wrote.' "The rich man replied, 'No, Father Abraham! But if someone is sent to them from the dead, then they will repent of their sins and turn to God.' "But Abraham said, 'If they won't listen to Moses and the prophets, they won't be persuaded even if someone rises from the dead.
— *Luke 16:19-31 (NLT)*

Heaven or Hell? A Personal Choice

The following are also words of Jesus Himself when He was teaching the people in the book of Matthew:

"Don't be afraid of those who want to kill your body; they cannot touch your soul. Fear only God, who can destroy both soul and body in hell."
— Matthew 10:28 (NLT)

"Then the King will turn to those on the left and say, 'Away with you, you cursed ones, into the eternal fire prepared for the devil and his demons. "And they will go away into eternal punishment, but the righteous will go into eternal life."
— Matthew 25:41, 46 (NLT)

Whenever the Bible talks about "the righteous", it is always referring to those who have placed their complete faith and trust in Jesus Christ as their Savior. They have been washed by the blood of the Lamb and their sins are totally forgiven. The righteousness of Christ is imputed to all who believe, because Jesus took upon Himself the sins of the whole world when He died on the cross. So, now when God looks at the believer, He sees only the righteousness of Jesus! That is what is known as the "beautiful exchange".

Sadly, the following are future events - at the very end of this age - culminating with the Great White Throne Judgement.

"And God will provide rest for you who are being persecuted and also for us when the Lord Jesus appears from heaven. He will come with his mighty angels, in flaming fire, bringing judgment on those who don't know God and on those who refuse to obey the Good News of our Lord Jesus. They will be

punished with eternal destruction, forever separated from the Lord and from his glorious power."
— 2 Thessalonians 1:7-9 (NLT)

"And I saw a great white throne and the one sitting on it. The earth and sky fled from his presence, but they found no place to hide. I saw the dead, both great and small, standing before God's throne. And the books were opened, including the Book of Life. And the dead were judged according to what they had done, as recorded in the books. The sea gave up its dead, and death and the grave gave up their dead. And all were judged according to their deeds. Then death and the grave were thrown into the lake of fire. This lake of fire is the second death. And anyone whose name was not found recorded in the Book of Life was thrown into the lake of fire."
— Revelation 20:11-15 (NLT)

Jesus longs for ALL of us to be well informed about Hell. He so wants us to make the right choice - and even tells us to - "choose life - for why would you perish?". He does not desire anyone to be lost and end up in Hell for all eternity! He has already paid the full price for all of us - so why in the world would anyone reject Him?

"The Lord isn't really being slow about his promise, as some people think. No, he is being patient for your sake. He does not want anyone to be destroyed, but wants everyone to repent."
— 2 Peter 3:9 (NLT)

He has made every provision for you and me to be saved and to be with Him for all eternity, but because we have free will, it is our choice. God doesn't send us to Hell - we choose to reject Him and His free gift to us, and instead, choose eternal separation from the God who so loves us. Sadly, the Bible says that the majority of people will choose to not believe and be separated from God forever.

"You can enter God's Kingdom only through the narrow gate. The highway to hell is broad, and its gate is wide for the many who choose that way. But the gateway to life is very narrow and the road is difficult, and only a few ever find it."
— *Matthew 7:13-14 (NLT)*

Now for the GOOD NEWS!

Jesus is the narrow gate!

Jesus said - "Yes, I am the gate. Those who come in through me will be saved. They will come and go freely and will find good pastures. The thief's purpose is to steal and kill and destroy. My purpose is to give them a rich and satisfying life. "I am the good shepherd. The good shepherd sacrifices his life for the sheep."
— *John 10:9-11 (NLT)*

THIS is the eternal reward for those who place their complete faith and trust in Jesus as their Savior. "

There is salvation in no one else! God has given no other name under heaven by which we must be saved."
— *Acts 4:12 (NLT)*

God gives us a small glimpse of what we are promised and will forever enjoy.

"Then the angel showed me a river with the water of life, clear as crystal, flowing from the throne of God and of the Lamb. It flowed down the center of the main street. On each side of the river grew a tree of life, bearing twelve crops of fruit, with a fresh crop each month. The leaves were used for medicine to heal the nations.

No longer will there be a curse upon anything. For the throne of God and of the Lamb will be there, and his servants will worship him. And they will see his face, and his name will be written on their foreheads.

And there will be no night there—no need for lamps or sun— for the Lord God will shine on them. And they will reign forever and ever.

Then the angel said to me, "Everything you have heard and seen is trustworthy and true. The Lord God, who inspires his prophets, has sent his angel to tell his servants what will happen soon."

"The Spirit and the bride say, "Come." Let anyone who hears this say, "Come." Let anyone who is thirsty, come. Let anyone who desires, drink freely from the water of life."
— *Revelation 22:1-6, 17 (NLT)*

"That is what the Scriptures mean when they say, "No eye has seen, no ear has heard, and no mind has imagined what God has prepared for those who love him."
— *1 Corinthians 2:9 (NLT)*

103

Those who have been washed in the blood of the Lamb - all believers - are also invited to the "Marriage Supper of the Lamb" - also known as the "Wedding Feast of the Lamb".

"Let us be glad and rejoice, and let us give honor to him. For the time has come for the wedding feast of the Lamb, and his bride has prepared herself. She has been given the finest of pure white linen to wear." For the fine linen represents the good deeds of God's holy people. And the angel said to me, "Write this: Blessed are those who are invited to the wedding feast of the Lamb." And he added, "These are true words that come from God."
— Revelation 19:7-9 (NLT)

Finally, Jesus will have restored ALL things back to their original intent - when God first created the perfect world and breathed life into Adam. Perfection at last, for all eternity! Never again will sin raise its ugly head or evil run rampant. Nothing that defiles will ever enter into the New Jerusalem that has come down out of Heaven!

Then I saw a new heaven and a new earth, for the old heaven and the old earth had disappeared! And the sea was also gone. And I saw the Holy City, the New Jerusalem, coming down from God out of heaven – like a bride beautifully dressed for her Husband."
— Revelation 21:1-2 (NLT)

"I heard a loud shout from the throne, saying, "Look, God's home is now among his people! He will live with them, and they will be his people. God himself will be with them. He will

wipe every tear from their eyes, and there will be no more death or sorrow or crying or pain. All these things are gone forever."

— Revelation 21:3-4 (NLT)

So tell me, my friend - which of these destinations would you desire to spend all eternity? Now that you know just who this Jesus is - **What is your choice?**

CONCLUSION

———————

So, Who is Jesus?

(Continued from the Preface)

When Jesus came to the region of Caesarea Philippi, He asked His disciples, "Who do people say that the Son of Man is?"

"Well", they replied, "some say John, the Baptist, some say Elijah, and others say Jeremiah or one of the other prophets."

Then He asked them, "But who do you say that I am?"

Simon Peter answered,

"You are the Messiah, the Son of the Living God!"

Jesus replied, "You are blessed, Simon, son of John, because my Father in heaven has revealed this to you. You did not learn this from any human being!"
— Matthew 16:13-17 (NLT)

So, Who is Jesus?

When the question arises, "Who is Jesus?", my heart and my thoughts are immediately flooded with everything that Jesus means to me.

Jesus is my Risen Savior and Lord! He is the Christ and my Promised Messiah! Jesus is my Redeemer, my Light and my Salvation, my Soon Coming King, and my Conquering King! He is the Lover of My Soul, my Bread of Life, my Living Water, my Good Shepherd, the Way, the Truth, and the Life, and my Everlasting Father! He is my Wonderful Counselor, my Mighty God, my Prince of Peace, my Sacrifice Lamb, and my Bright and Morning Star! Jesus is the Creator of All Things, the Word of God Become Flesh, my God of Love, my God of Mercy, and my God of Grace! He is my God of Forgiveness, the Perfect Relational God – Father, Son, and Holy Spirit! Jesus is the Restoration of All Things! He is my Loving Bridegroom and my Divine Romance! Jesus is my Everything!

My friend, I truly hope and pray that as you have been searching this all out, that God's Spirit has touched your heart and illuminated your way. I pray that He has made this Jesus so very, very real to you. Jesus so loves you and has paid a great, great price – His precious blood – for you to enjoy Him for all eternity.

Right now, will you ask God to forgive you and to cleanse you of all your sin? Ask Him to wash you with the precious blood of Jesus and come into your heart – into your life – to change you and make you a new person. Confess out of your mouth that Jesus Christ is Lord and that you truly believe that God has raised Him from the dead.

108

God has made a huge promise to you in His Word – and He honors His Word above His Name.

He promises that –

If you confess with your mouth that Jesus is Lord and believe in your heart that God raised Him from the dead, you will be saved! For it is by believing in your heart that you are made right with God, and it is by confessing with your mouth that you are saved. As the Scriptures tell us, "Anyone who trusts in Him will never be disgraced. Jew and Gentile are the same in this respect. They have the same Lord, who gives generously to all who call on Him. For everyone who calls on the name of the Lord will be saved.
— *Romans 10:9-13 (NLT)*

The next time you are asked, "Who is Jesus?", may your redeemed, born-again heart be flooded with the emotion and the reality of how great this Jesus truly is!

"Therefore if anyone is in Christ, he is a new creation; old things have passed away; behold, all things have become new."
— *2 Corinthians 5:17 (NASB)*

"May Jesus become and remain your greatest Treasure!"

EPILOGUE

The Beautiful Plan of Salvation

PROCLAIMING THE GOSPEL or the GOOD NEWS OF JESUS!

Are you now wondering, How can I be saved - or - born-again? Jesus Himself said: *"Truly truly I say to you, unless one is born again, he cannot see the Kingdom of God. Do not be amazed that I said to you - You must be born again"*
— *John 3:3, 7 (NASB)*

Romans tells us: ***"for all have sinned and fall short of the glory of God,"***.
— *Romans 3:23 (NASB)*

So every person who has ever lived has sinned - so, we ALL stand GUILTY before God.

Romans 6:23 teaches us:

"For the wages of sin is death, but the free gift of God is eternal life in Christ Jesus our Lord."
— *Romans 6:23 (NASB)*

Epilogue

Because of our sinful lives, we all have earned and deserve total separation from God in hell. Jesus taught often about an eternal hell. Hell is our default destination UNLESS we turn to Jesus in faith and repentance.

Romans shows us:

"But God demonstrates His own love toward us, in that while we were yet sinners, Christ died for us. Much more then, having now been justified by His blood, we shall be saved from the wrath of God through Him."
— *Romans 5:8-9 (NASB)*

This is what is known as the "beautiful exchange" - Jesus took our sins upon Himself in order to pay the price for us on the cross - He, in exchange, gave us His righteousness - we receive this by faith.

The Gospel of John declares:

"But as many as received Him, to them He gave the right to become children of God, even to those who believe in His name,".
— *John 1:12 (NASB)*

It is in the turning from your sinful ways the best you know how - which is repentance - and the receiving of Jesus as Lord and Savior that the Holy Spirit gives you the power to become a son or a daughter of God.

In the Book of Acts:

"Peter said to them, "Repent, and each of you be baptized in the name of Jesus Christ for the forgiveness of your sins; and you will receive the gift of the Holy Spirit."
— *Acts 2:38 (NASB)*

Ephesians declares this beautiful truth:

"For by grace you have been saved through faith; and that not of yourselves, it is the gift of God; not as a result of works, so that no one may boast."
— *Ephesians 2:8-9 (NASB)*

Romans urges us to confess with our mouth and believe with our heart!

"But what does it say? "The word is near you, in your mouth and in your heart"—that is, the word of faith which we are preaching, that if you confess with your mouth Jesus as Lord, and believe in your heart that God raised Him from the dead, you will be saved; for with the heart a person believes, resulting in righteousness, and with the mouth he confesses, resulting in salvation." "For the Scripture says, "Whoever believes in Him will not be disappointed." For there is no distinction between Jew and Greek; for the same Lord is Lord of all, abounding in riches for all who call on Him; for "Whoever will call on the name of the Lord will be saved."
— *Romans 10:8-13 (NASB)*

1 John tells us of the amazing confidence that we can have in Jesus and His beautiful offer of salvation!

Epilogue

"These things I have written to you who believe in the name of the Son of God, so that you may know that you have eternal life."
— *1 John 5:13 (NASB)*

You can KNOW for SURE! How beautiful is that?! As you can see, Jesus has done absolutely everything needed for our salvation. We just need to get our hearts in line with Him, believe, receive Him, and then follow Him!

Friend, humbly cry out to God, confessing and asking Him to forgive you of all of your sins. Turn from your sinful ways the best you know how and ask Jesus to come into your heart and life and save you. By faith receive Him and begin living your life to please Him. God's Word says: Therefore if anyone is in Christ, he is a new creature; the old things passed away; behold, new things have come. You will find your desires and whole philosophy of life starting to change. **YOU ARE A NEW PERSON - YOU HAVE BEEN BORN AGAIN!** This is the greatest miracle anyone could ever experience.

"For God so loved the world, that He gave His only begotten Son, that whoever believes in Him will not perish, but have eternal life.
— *John 3:16 (NASB)*

And finally, I would like to end with the promise of this mystery made known - this beautiful miracle - one more time!

"Therefore if anyone is in Christ, he is a new creation; old things have passed away; behold, all things have become new.
— 2 Corinthians 5:17 (NASB)

JUST THE BEGINNING!

115

(A VISION ~ A POEM)

Redemption

On this most blessed of all nights, in the city of Bethlehem, our beautiful Savior is born - for in this heavenly vision, I see Him wrapped in a cloth lying in a manger. Heaven is rejoicing, as myriads of angels fill the sky in praise, adoration, and worship! There are kings giving gifts of gold, frankincense, and myrrh. Shepherds and wisemen are bowing down in pure adoration and worship of this Child! What manner of Child could this be?!

But wait! In this vision, years later, I see this same Babe, who is wrapped in a cloth and lying in that manger - but instead - He is wrapped in a blood stained cloth, lying in a cold dark tomb! What have they done??? Could they have killed the Lord of Glory - the very One who came to save them?!?

Oh, but look!! Now I see a bright light bursting forth from this cold, dark tomb - the stone has been rolled away! There is no body!!! But I do see that blood stained cloth lying there and the bloody napkin that embraced my Savior's head - folded neatly and lying where His head used to lay!

They say that folded napkin is a PROMISE that He is coming back for the ones that He has died to save! He has risen – just like He said He would!!! Hallelujah!!! Praise our God and King forever and ever!!! Truly Christmas has come – and truly Easter has provided that it will remain forever! Our Christ – He is King!

We hold on firmly to this Blessed Hope - for Jesus is coming back to receive us to Himself – that where He is, there we may be also – forever!!!

~ RANDY GENTILLE

Other published works of the author include, "The Father's Love" album, which was released on August 2, 2021. All of which are original songs that also magnify Jesus and declare who He is. They are a Proclamation of the Gospel or the Good News of Jesus!

http://randygentille.hearnow.com
(Website link)

**The "JESUS Who is He?" paperback and e-book and "The Father's Love" CD and digital album are all available on Amazon.

JESUS

Who is He?

Who is He - to you?

Savior or Judge?

Heaven
or
Hell?

A reality that each and every one of us
will experience soon - a reality that is

~ just a heartbeat away ~

Our life is like a vapor - that appears for
a little while - and then - vanishes!

BE WISE - BE PREPARED NOW!

"May Jesus become and remain your greatest Treasure"

Made in the USA
Columbia, SC
03 July 2024

37988115R00074